Sermons
for Celebrating

Landrum P. Leavell

Broadman Press
Nashville, Tennessee

© Copyright 1978 • Broadman Press
All rights reserved.

4222–31
ISBN: 0-8054-2231-5

Dewey Decimal Classification: 252
Subject Heading: SERMONS

Library of Congress Catalog Card Number: 77–090220
Printed in the United States of America

Preface

For the thirty years since my ordination to the gospel ministry, preaching has been the consuming interest of my life. Not only does preaching give me a deep sense of fulfillment in respect to God's call for my life but also I have found genuine worship experiences in my study as I prepared to preach.

The most perplexing, continuing problem I faced in sermon preparation centered in the special occasions to which I wanted to apply the gospel. It is both challenging and frustrating to try to present the unchanged and unchanging Christmas message for the same occasions in a new and different way over several decades.

This volume grew out of that problem and is a compilation of a number of these sermons used on special Sundays. It is offered with the prayer that fellow preachers will find these sermons of help in planning and preparing for those significant special days.

LANDRUM P. LEAVELL

Contents

Dedication

To my preacher brethren
who faithfully preach the Word
in season and out of season.

May their tribe increase!

1. Goals for Growth

2 Peter 3:18

Many large industries today utilize what is called a goal-oriented approach to management. Simply put, this means they determine where they are and where they want to go; then in keeping with those desired destinations, they set goals which lead to reaching the destination. They bring into play all the resources of the organization for the achievement of those goals. This is an excellent way, as experience has shown, for big business to operate.

It is my judgment that the goal-oriented approach is not only viable in big business but is also a very practical method on an individual basis. This approach to the ministry of the church has revitalized a large number of churches across the nation. It is determined on the basis of Christ's teachings in the New Testament that a church exists in a community for one major reason. The prime reason for existence, the *raison d'etre*, is to reach people for Christ. When that determination is made, a church can focus all its energies in the direction of reaching people. Birth in Christ precedes growth in Christ.

This is not only true and workable for big business and a church but it will also work in the life of an individual. This is just as true for you individually as it is for

General Motors or First Baptist Church. Without hesitancy I underwrite, approve, and commend New Year's resolutions. Some cynically state they "go in one year and out the other," but that's not always true. If you make New Year's resolutions out of a deep sense of commitment to Jesus Christ and in keeping with Christ-honoring goals in daily living, then these are good; they can be helpful and increase the effectiveness of your daily witness.

If you fail to set goals for yourself, it's hardly possible you will achieve anything worthwhile. I can hardly imagine Tom Landry, head coach of the Dallas Cowboys, saying to his football team, "We're not going to set any goals for next year. I believe it's bad psychology to set goals and not reach them. So, fellows, we're all just going out there and see what happens." Now is that the approach Coach Landry takes? Not on the basis of the reports I've received!

I can't imagine a sales manager entering a meeting with his salemen and saying, "Now, fellows, you can relax. We don't have any goals for sales next year. Just forget about it. Go out there and enjoy salesmanship, but let's not try to accomplish anything measurable or tangible." A sales manager tries to challenge and motivate salesmen on the basis of goals that are possible impossibilities. They are things which can be done if each does his best. With that sort of challenge and motivation they go out.

The next year is the first year of the rest of your life. It can be a year of decision. It can be a year of spiritual growth. If we ever intend to achieve more in the future than we have previously, resolutions can form the tracks upon which we place our lives and aim toward a target.

What are some steps in establishing New Year's resolutions? I want to suggest three that may be helpful for you. The first is to

Turn.

That's rather simple, isn't it? T-u-r-n. Now frankly, if you're content with life as it's now being lived, if you've made your mark, found your niche, and don't want to be disturbed, these words will have no meaning for you. You might as well be doing something else. But if there is discontent in your life regarding your witness for the Lord Jesus, and if you are aware of the fact that you have not begun to measure up to your potential, then perhaps something you read will be helpful.

I've had to face the fact on occasion that some people don't want to turn. Some don't want to change. Some people don't want to be happy. I encounter these individuals periodically and find them, in the main, to be people who have a very strong sense of guilt. They feel they ought to be punished for what they've done; so they hold on to their misery, unhappiness, and discontent, feeling this is no more than they deserve. They remain unhappy through life. But for those who seek a fuller life and wider service for Christ, I remind you, there will be no spiritual growth as long as you are holding on to known sin.

The Greek word for *repent* literally means to "turn around." That's what it's all about. If you have any desire to be more like Christ, it involves turning around. If you have no desire in your heart to be more like the Master, there's something tragically missing in the experience you claim. You may be claiming church membership when that has little to do with your salvation relationship in Christ at the beginning. You see, salvation is not synonymous with church membership. You may be a church member in good standing, with your pledge paid in full, but if you have no desire to be more like Jesus, something is wrong. Maybe the missing ingredient is conversion. That involves a transformation which Paul described as old things passing away and all things becoming new. In that radical transformation there is implanted in the heart a desire to be like Jesus.

I'm presuming that you want to be like Christ, therefore I'm suggesting that the first step to a more Christlike life is to turn, to turn from every known sin, every area of dishonesty, everything immoral, little, or self-defeating.

There are a number of pilots whom I claim as friends, I suppose two score or more. I've had the opportunity of flying with many of them and have discovered there are two things a pilot has to know in charting a course. You already know these. He has to know where he is and where he wants to go! That's trite, but it's just as applicable in our lives as Christians as it is for pilots who want to fly from one place to another. We must know where we are and where we want to go.

Repentance is the first of these steps; for repentance not only involves turning but is also an admission of who we are in facing every known sin. When you establish that point of reference, you're ready to begin to move toward a given destination. You can't seek a destination until you have a starting point. If our destination is to reveal Christ in daily living, everyone of us, if honest, must admit that we have a long way to go. There's so much about our lives not like Jesus.

Maybe someone says, "I've never committed any of

the gross sins." I'm willing to concede that, for there are many moral, high-principled persons in society. But the fact of the matter is gross sins are not the only sins.

Maybe you've never committed a crime for which you could be convicted by a judge and jury and sentenced to jail. Perhaps not, but neither did Judas. Judas never did anything for which he could have been sentenced to imprisonment. All he ever did was betray a friend. He played out his true role, that of a money-loving materialist. When it came to a choice between this friend Jesus and thirty pieces of silver, he chose what he loved most. He chose silver. Now if that were a crime, our courts would be far more overcrowded than they are. However, it wasn't a crime for which he could be convicted in an open court.

You and I, though we've never been guilty of some of the so-called gross sins, are nevertheless guilty sinners. We betray Jesus Christ with an un-Christlike spirit. Maybe it's hostility. Maybe it's bitterness. Maybe it's animosity or grudge bearing. There's nothing that so quickly negates your Christian testimony as an un-Christlike spirit.

Perhaps you feel you just can't forget what's been done to you, that you'll never be able to get over it unless this other person takes certain steps in the sequence you've preestablished. Now if he will do this, this, and this, then maybe he can be forgiven. Let me remind you of what Jesus said. When the disciples came and asked, "Lord, teach us to pray," remember how he answered? He said, "In this manner pray ye . . . forgive us our debts as we forgive our debtors" (Matt. 6:9–12). Now, brother, that's important. You had better listen to that. Forgive us *as* we forgive others. From

the very instant you become unwilling to forgive someone else, in that instant you cut off access to God's forgiveness in your life.

Remember the parable Jesus gave. He told us about
a fellow who owed another man over one million dollars
in today's currency. This guy had a run of bad luck,
he had had short crops, maybe a long dry season. He
wasn't able to grow enough wheat when it came time
to make a payment on his debt. He didn't have the
money. He went in to the king he owed, sat down, and
explained his plight. "I don't have it, but I know I owe
it, and if you'll extend the time a little, I'm going to
pay this debt. I've come to ask for mercy." Instead of
mercy, do you remember what the king did? He said,
"I see the sincerity you've displayed. I'm going to mark
that debt paid in full." The fellow couldn't believe it.
He jumped out of his chair, ran around, hugged the
king, and flew out into the street looking for someone
to share the good news. He looked up and down, and
all of a sudden his eye began to narrow and his mouth
became a straight line.

He walked over to a man huddled in his rags, obvi-
ously a poor man, grabbed him by his lapels, and began
to shake him. He said, "Hey, have you forgotten that
$17.65 you owe me?" The poor fellow looked up and
replied, "I've been looking for you. I want to tell you
I've had some bad luck. My wife's been in the hospital,
I've got doctor bills, the kids have been sick, and I
haven't been able to work. I've been down with pleurisy
and arthritis and nothing's gone right. I haven't been
able to work, but I wanted to tell you if you'll give me
a little time, I'm going to pay that $17.65." That fellow
who had just been forgiven a one million dollar debt

said, "Oh, no you don't. You're going to jail!"

Do you remember that story? (Matt. 18:21–30). That's not exactly like Jesus told it, yet that's the spirit of it. That's precisely what Jesus meant. He put you and me in the category of owing one million dollars in sin and being forgiven by the goodness of God. Then, in our littleness and un-Christlikeness, we say to some other human being who had ruffled our feelings, or who said something we didn't like, "I'll not forgive you."

How do we betray Jesus? We can betray him with an un-Christlike spirit. The sins of the spirit are sins just as much as adultery, fornication, lying, drunkenness, stealing, or any other sin that we consider heinous. It's just as reprehensible to be guilty of the sins of the spirit in the sight of God. That's what the Sermon on the Mount is about. It's as bad to hate as it is to kill. I didn't say it, Jesus did! He said it is just as bad to lust in your mind and build up pictures in your fantasies and daydreams as it is to commit an overt act of adultery. Jesus said it. That's a sin of the spirit, and it's equated with the sin of the flesh.

Turning involves an admission that we are wrong and asking God to forgive us as we forgive our debtors. When we are forgiving them, forgiveness becomes a two-way street. Forgiveness comes to us and goes out from us. There's no such thing as forgiveness coming to us and stopping. When you cut off the channel by which forgiveness flows through you, you've stopped it. It won't come to you.

A very vital aspect of turning is to extend forgiveness to anyone who needs it. We have to give it to get it. Someone has suggested we ought to change our "drop dead list" to a "prayer list." Do you have a drop dead list? Let me urge you to begin to pray for those folks, for God loves them. He loves them just as much as he loves you. He loves that lost man just as much as he loves those of us in church. He doesn't love us any more because we are faithful than he loves the lost man who hasn't yet found him. He loves us all.

The second step in setting new resolutions is to

Try.

If you establish some goals for growth, this is a must.

The neurotic person says, "I wish I were Abraham Lincoln." The crazy person says, "I am Abraham Lincoln." The healthy person says, "I am who I am, and you are who you are." How much time have you wasted in life wondering what you could do if you had the money Mr. Rich has? Or if you had the talents of Billy Graham? Oh, what glorious things you could do if you had what they have!

The healthy person comes to grips with the fact that he is who he is and accepts himself like that, a combination of strengths and weaknesses. We are all a mixture of these. No one is without weakness. No one is without strengths. The fact for emphasis is God accepts you just as you are, for who you are, and therefore you can accept yourself. You don't have to be somebody else for God to love you. God loves you like you are. He made you. He put you here, so accept yourself.

Noninvolvement has been defined as the urban syndrome. *Syndrome* is a medical term defined as the aggregate of concurrent symptoms indicating an abnormality. Let us be reminded that noninvolvement is an abnormality. Withdrawal from voluntary responsibility is the modern social disease threatening our society. This has touched a lot of different areas, but in no area is it more acute than in the work of the kingdom of God. The only known cure for noninvolvement is involvement.

Let me remind you of another little vignette from the life of Jesus. Do you recall that one day, when he and his disciples were walking along a road, he saw a fig tree that had no fruit? He pronounced a curse upon the tree, and it withered and died. Jesus did not consider the tree superfluous because it produced rotten fruit, or because the fruit was too small, or because the fruit didn't measure up to some standard. That tree was determined to be superfluous because it had no fruit.

Have you noticed the relationship in life between fruitlessness and criticism? Fruitbearers, who are designed to bear a harvest, a crop, who do not produce a crop become faultfinders. This is true in the whole spectrum of community life. It's true in the church. We try to justify our noninvolvement by our criticism of those who are involved, active, and are trying to be fruitful.

Hear someone who says, "I am unhappy in my church; therefore, I won't give any money." Another says, "I'm unhappy in my church, so I won't work. I refuse to teach or serve." Another says, "I'm unhappy in my church; therefore, I won't witness." Soon that vicious circle drags one down. The cause of fruitlessness is unhappiness, and unhappiness is inseparably connected with the fruitlessness. It looks like we could understand that, doesn't it? Establish your goals for growth. Say, "I will try." You don't have to produce the biggest harvest being produced, but if you try and produce some harvest, that's superior to nothing. Jesus cursed the barren fig tree. No fruit. The tree didn't produce small fruit or bitter fruit—no fruit!

A third step toward successful resolution is to

Trust.

This includes the conviction that God has something for us better than what we now have. Do we believe that? No, we don't believe it. We don't believe that heaven is going to be better than what we've got on earth. We like what we have here so well we don't think anything can beat it. That's why we're not homesick!

We don't even believe that God can compensate for our giving up certain sins which we have fallen in love with. If you're frustrated and empty on the inside and know you are leading a meaningless, meandering life, God has something better for you!

If you're a young person, you can make the vow Daniel made: "I will not defile myself." (Dan. 1:8). If you're a family man, you can make the vow Joshua made, saying it didn't matter what the rest of the world did: "As for me and my house, we will serve the Lord" (Josh. 24:15). If you're a young businessman, you can make the vow Jacob made, "Of all that thou shalt give me I will surely give the tenth unto thee" (Gen. 28:22).

Goals for growth are under consideration, but try to keep in mind the high cost of noninvolvement and failure to establish goals. Jesus said, "If any man would save his life," that is, keep it to himself through noninvolvement, "he will lose it." But he also said, "If any man will lose his life," by involvement in the lives of other people, "he will save it" (Matt. 16:25). That's pretty important, isn't it? One of the paradoxes of the kingdom is that you save your life when you lose it. Jesus said that and the reason he could say it is because he's the judge. He's the one before whom we will stand in the final day of reckoning.

You know, the judge on that occasion is not going to be interested primarily in the amount of your growth. He's not going to measure you and say, "You grew fourteen inches," and measure someone else and say, "He didn't grow but twelve inches," and measure another and say, "He grew twenty inches." That's not the important thing. The important thing in the day of judgment is direction. The question won't be how far did you travel, but what was your goal, where were you going, which way were you heading? You cannot be heading toward Christ and away from him at the same time. He that is not with Christ is against him.

Some of us ought to resolve to become involved— right now. You are doing absolutely nothing spiritually. You are not happy in your Christian life. You have not experienced one iota of growth because you are not facing the right direction. Your spiritual life is stagnant, not because Christ wants it to be, but because you won't let it grow. You are the only one who can change that.

Maybe you ought to say, "I'll volunteer. I'll drive a bus. I'll become a bus pastor. I'll take a Sunday School class. I'll accept a committee responsibility and use what talent I have for Christ and for his kingdom. I'll do anything I'm asked to do. I'm available." Now, friend, if you are willing to lose your life in that way and to alter your schedule at personal sacrifice, I can guarantee you've stepped upon the highway of growth.

You don't have any idea what God can do for you and through you in the new year if you are only willing. This is the hour for all of us, as spectators, to get out of the grandstand and into the ball game. When you put on the pads and uniform and get into the ball game, you may get bumped around a little, but that's a whole lot more fun than sitting in the grandstand and not being a part of the action. That's the decision facing us, are we going to be spectators or participants? There's a song we used to sing when I was a teenager, and the chorus went like this:

> "If you can't preach like Peter, If you can't pray like Paul,
> You can tell the love of Jesus, And say, he died for all."

That's it. You don't have to be able to preach like Billy Graham. You don't have to be able to teach like the finest Bible scholars, but you can tell the love of Jesus and say he died for all. Are you willing to get involved?

We have reached the time when we must make the decision either to be involved or not involved. It's the difference between saving life or losing it. If you're going to save it, you've got to lose it; but if you are trying to save it, then you are going to lose it after all. Now is the time. You make the decision. I have done the part that God called me to do. Now you have to do the part he's calling you to do.

2. The Neglected Revival
Luke 6:38

Across the years we have experienced many and varied revivals in our Baptist fellowship. We've seen the mighty wonder-working power of God in our midst. We've witnessed scores and hundreds brought to Christ for salvation through faith in his name. We've known every kind of revival imaginable, save one. This is the revival that comes when God's people individually get right with God financially. We really have not had that revival.

In our church today, approximately one out of every four members makes no contribution of record. Can you believe that? Of the remainder who do contribute, approximately one fourth contribute less than fifty cents a week to the work of the kingdom of God through this church. That means that about one out of every two members gives nothing or a mere pittance to the most important business on the face of the earth, the kingdom of God.

We have eyes with which to see. We have ears with which to hear, but the tragedy of all tragedies is that we appear to be both blind and deaf. We're unable to evaluate the truths so evident to us. We hear with our ears but have no comprehension and perception. With lesson after lesson staring us in the face, we have not yet grasped the relationship between affluence and discontent. The more we have, the more we want. The more we have, the unhappier we become. This lesson is clear for all who have eyes to see, but in our hardness of heart we refuse to learn. *Things* cannot provide the satisfaction they promise. The person who cannot be happy without money will never be happy with money.

If the girl or boy you are dating is a gold digger, you'd be well advised to leave him or her and look for another. If they are not happy without money, I've got news for you! They'll never be happy with money. Any human being could recall illustration after illustration of that truth. We have eyes, we have ears; yet we are blind and deaf to the lessons of life.

Just a periodic, cursory perusal of the newspapers would lead one to conclude that wealth does not create happiness. The people whose names appear in boldface type—the miserable, unhappy, divorced time and again—are the wealthier people of our land, saying to us in deeds more eloquent than words, "Money is not where it's *at!* Money is not the answer."

God never intended things to be collected. The wisdom of God is that things are to be used. Man in his perversity has distorted the plan of God. God's plan is that we use things and love people. Not us. We prefer to love things and use people. We set about to accomplish that intention in our lives. God did not intend or design man to be a reservoir. He intended man to be a channel. When we become savings accounts rather than checking accounts, we have turned from the purpose of Almighty God. Real revival will be experienced when God's people get right with God financially and invest his tithe in his storehouse, his church.

I want you to look at three things with me: the place, the power, and the potential of money. What is its

Place?

In our lives money has priority. Top priority is the place it holds. Most of our minds are dazzled by the "great god, cash." The glitter of gold has blinded us to eternal values. It's been said that money talks. I've never heard a dollar bill say a word, but I've heard money talk. It tells the story of penury and plenty, of greed and generosity. The money that comes through your hands talks and tells exactly what your life-style is. It says worlds about your relationship to Jesus Christ. The quantity of money you possess doesn't affect the issue.

Because we've given money top priority, we've afforded recognition to those who have the most of it. What ideals do we hold up to our younger generation? When we tell them of the experience of some person after whom we would like them to pattern their lives, invariably it's someone who has succeeded financially. That's the way man thinks, but that's not God's way of thinking.

We tend to forget that a human being of humble circumstances may well be the most successful person of all in the sight of God. Take John the Baptist. He didn't have any of this world's goods, but Jesus said about John, "Among them that are born of women there hath not risen a greater than John the Baptist" (Matt. 11:11). I doubt if he could buy a meal in a local restaurant if he were here today, and in the same financial position he was in during his lifetime.

Do you remember the little woman who put in her offering at the Temple? It's strange, for those who don't believe in storehouse tithing, that Jesus commended the woman for putting it in the right place. He commended the little widow who didn't have much, but who gave all she had. And she put it in the right place. He said of all that the rich people had given, nobody equaled the gift this little lady gave. You see, in God's sight the richest are not necessarily the most righteous. They could be, and by God's grace they ought to be, but they aren't always. Sometimes the poorest are the ones whom God commends.

Money holds a place. It's a place parallel to personality. Your dollars, your bank account, your oil leases, your stocks and bonds are not just cold cash and filthy lucre. Your income represents you; for it takes you to earn a livelihood. It demands the utilization of your eyes, your ears, your mouth, your nose, your hands, your arms, your body, your mind. You invest everything you have and are to make your income; so your income is translated personality. It's you! Brother, when you withhold your money from the kingdom of God and from the use of the Lord Jesus, you're withholding yourself. When you say, "I am too poor to tithe," and "I can't give," you are saying, "God can have none of me!" Money is parallel to personality because it takes your personality to make your living.

Man confuses this issue. We can easily come to think of money as an end. Jesus knew that. That's why he constantly exalted personality or humanity; for he never intended us to become slaves to money, but slaves to God. In our hardness of heart we bow our knees in obeisance to the great god, cash. Jesus wanted us to exalt humanity, not possessions, because people are important, not things.

Jesus asked, "What shall it profit a man, if he shall gain the whole world, and lose his own soul?" (Mark 8:36). What difference would it make if you were as rich as J. Paul Getty, yet die and go to hell? What good can your money do you then? None. Jesus tried continuously to tell us that personality is more important than possessions. But there are many people who, in their covetousness and greed, will sit back and say, "The New Testament doesn't say much about money." Brother, don't show your ignorance, for that's what it is. There's no other word for it. Out of the thirty-eight parables of Jesus, sixteen of them, or almost half, have to do with the stewardship of material possessions. And you don't think the New Testament has anything to say about stewardship? That's mainly what Jesus talked about. The value of human personality is to be exalted above all other values because people are all that will populate heaven. Nothing else is going to make it. You are not going to take your bank account, your stocks and bonds, and your other holdings. You are not going to take your house. You are not going to take your front yard!

You know, some people are strange! They spend the Lord's Day working on their front yards! They have the most beautiful yards in town, but their spiritual lives are disreputable! You're not going to get to heaven on that front yard. There isn't but one thing going to populate heaven, and that's people, people who have a right relationship with God.

I know some folks don't like this kind of talk, but they are the very ones who need this neglected revival. The ones who fuss about it are the ones who need it the most.

I like to pause periodically and reflect on the truth

that there's only one thing about which two Baptists can agree. That's how much money a third Baptist ought to give! We may not be in agreement, but, friend, if you want to disagree, you are going to have to disagree with the gospel and Jesus Christ. You cannot define life in terms of "my goods."

The place money holds is a potential for partnership. Money is not evil in itself; it's amoral. It is the use to which we put money that becomes evil. Money has an equal potential for righteousness for it can bring us into partnership with God.

I don't know of any sane person who thinks of money as an end in itself. Sane people all understand that money is a means to an end. The big question is, What is the end to which money is a means? Most everyone says, "I just want enough to provide security in my old age. I just want to get my kids educated and have enough to live on in retirement." Now, you can talk to the richest or the poorest, and everyone says the same thing. That's all anybody wants!

Then the question comes, How much is it going to take to accomplish this? No one knows for sure. Jesus Christ is the only security, the only source of peace of mind for a human being. Brother, if the only security you've got is in a bank account, I want to remind you it can be wiped out in the twinkling of an eye. If you don't believe it, ask the folks who were around in 1929. If all the security you've got is in this world's goods, you don't have security. One little war, one little depression, or continued inflation can eat up that which you thought provided security.

Your money may buy you membership in exclusive

clubs, but only a partnership with God can get you through the pearly gates.

Let's look at money and

Power.

What kind of power does money have? It has the power of possessiveness. Like the rich fool in Jesus' parable we come to say, "My barns, my crops, my soul."

If you want to see something interesting, just notice the number of times a kid, a little kid, uses the first personal pronouns. "Mine, my hat, my toys, that's mine, give it to me." We grow up physically but never spiritually, still holding on to these things, saying, "My, my, my, mine, mine, mine."

Money deceives and deludes us, for it makes us think of life in relation to the abundance of things we possess. That was precisely the problem of the rich fool in the parable of Jesus. Men forget everything in the pursuit of wealth. They give all they have and are to gain what the world offers. They find to their dismay and eternal chagrin that their only claim to fame is that their mortal remains are the richest ones in a given cemetery. You can't take it with you, but thank God you can send it on ahead. You can lay up treasure in heaven where moth and rust never corrupt.

When a young Methodist preacher preached his first sermon, his subject was "God Owns Everything." He took as his text, "The earth is the Lord's, and the fulness thereof; the world, and they that dwell therein" (Ps. 24:1). As the service ended in the small rural church where he was preaching, the richest man in the community came by and said, "Son, I want to talk with you this afternoon." The young preacher said, "Fine." They made an arrangement to meet.

The rich man met the young preacher, and they started on a ride, up one road and down another, the rich man pointing on both sides of the road, "That's my field. Those are my pastures. Those cattle belong to me. These are my houses. Those are my barns. Those horses over there belong to me. These beautiful crops here are all mine." Mile after mile they rode. After several hours of riding and displaying all he had, the rich man brought the young preacher back to the church and before he let him out said, "Now, son, don't you ever preach that sermon again. I've shown you today that God doesn't own everything, for these things are mine." With a burst of divine insight the young preacher smiled and answered, "Sir, we can't settle this question today, but I have a suggestion. If you will, let's just make an agreement to meet back here on this same spot one hundred years from today and then decide." Isn't it interesting how captivated we are with things that are temporal and how turned off we are by some things that are eternal.

Money has the power of prejudice. It can make us indifferent to the needs of other people. The rich young ruler was content with what he had. He had no disposition to sell anything or to give anything away to poor people. Now, that didn't lessen the need of the poor people, it merely showed what kind of person he was. He didn't care.

Paradoxically, extreme wealth and extreme poverty produce the same evil. Extreme wealth and extreme poverty both lead to starvation of the soul. It's easy for the rich man to seclude himself, surrounded by his possessions, and say, "Soul, take thine ease, eat, drink and be merry, for tomorrow I may die." But it's also easy for the poverty-stricken person to see nothing but his poverty and need and to become lazy and dependent upon society, a recipient of welfare. So it works the same way at both ends of the spectrum.

Money has the power of propagation, for we can use it to spread the gospel and prepare the world for the coming of Christ and the judgment of God upon the sins of men. Statistics show that more money is spent every year for Christmas tree decorations than Southern Baptists give for all mission causes. What a commentary on life in the twentieth century! It would be funny if it weren't tragic.

Money also has

Potential.

It has the potential of portraying our passion. We can show by the way that we spend our money what we really love. Jesus said, "Where your treasure is, there will your heart be also" (Matt. 6:21).

You can reverse that equation. Where your heart is, your treasure will be. Friend, if you haven't put anything in the church of a material nature, your heart is not in it. Don't tell me you love the church. Don't tell me how much you love Christ and his church. If you have not made any investment in the work of his kingdom through his church, you've told the world what you really love, and it's not the church.

A proverb says, "A fool and his money are soon parted." But you can paraphrase that, "A Christian and his money are soon shared." A very prominent feature of apostolic Christianity was a passion for the lost. It

was so great, so consuming that the apostles were willing
to sell all their possessions and invest all their money
in the work of the kingdom through the church. Their
passion remains as an example to us.

You know, there are a lot of people who get hung
up on this 10 percent and never see the truth of the
gospel. The gospel demand is for 100 percent! Jesus
demands our all! We stumble along, unable to step over
the molehill of 10 percent; therefore, we never approach
the mountain of 100 percent. If the world is going to
know the power of the gospel and our love for Christ,
our material assets must be surrendered to him for his
direction.

Money has the potential of enabling us to practice
our passion. With our money we put feet to our prayers.
We've just said through our church, or at least some
have, "We believe in foreign missions. We believe in
it by a special offering amounting to over sixteen thousand dollars." We believe in it. We've proven that belief
by our giving. This amounts to putting up and not shut-
ting up.

We've outlived the day when people are going to act
on our words alone. People are not going to be impressed by anything other than our practice. When we
practice what we preach, the lost will sit up and take
notice. If we believe that the kingdom of God is to be
sought above all, then the kingdom has to be first. Christ
must control our cash as well as our time and our talents.
Christian giving is to be the external manifestation of
our attitude toward life. It is merely the economic result
of a spiritual transformation. If that result is not in evi-
dence, there is real doubt about the transformation.

This potential is the opportunity to perpetuate our passion. In other words, we can give permanence to what we believe by the money we invest. If you believe in the church, then invest to perpetuate it. If you believe in a lot of things other than the church, you have the right to choose them. But if you are a Christian and know what it means to put Christ first, then his church is the most important institution on the face of the earth! It's the only one about which Jesus said, "The gates of hell shall not prevail against it" (Matt. 16:18). If you believe that, then you'd better make your investment in the eternal institution. It is the only investment that's going to pay dividends eternally. Any other investment is going to turn to ashes and will equal nothing. We can, through the ministry of our local church, prove to unborn generations what we think of the kingdom. We can do it by the buildings we build and the victories that are won in Christ's power. They will stand as mute testimony of our love for Jesus and our commitment to things that are everlasting.

King Louis XI of France, in a moment when he thought himself to be the most pious, made a "solemn deed and covenant" conveying the entire French province of Boulogne to the virgin Mary. Boy, wasn't that a magnanimous gift? He gave her the whole province. She was long since dead, but this was his way of saying what he believed. In small print in that covenant, which was supposed to be a pledge of the love of Louis XI to the virgin Mary, he reserved "all the revenues thereof" for himself. Big deal. He really made a contribution to the kingdom of God, didn't he? He gave Mary the whole province but kept the money. What did she have when she had the province? I wonder what God thought of the childishness of the king of France when he made that gift.

I can imagine God must weep in brokenhearted anguish at the childishness of his followers in every generation who say, "Lord, I love you. Lord, I give you my life, but I reserve my money. I'm not going to give you my money. Just my life." What does he have when he has your life and not your money? He doesn't have you. He doesn't have you until you give him the totality of your being. All that you have, all that you are, all that you own, and all that you ever will own—that's when he has you and that's when your gift to him has significance.

3. What's God Saying?

John 20:11-18

Some time ago a prominent public official said we had reached the time in our nation when we needed to lower our voices, stop shouting, and listen to one another. Society is filled with a cacophony; shrill, strident, militant, hungry, greedy, impoverished voices all comprise the sound we hear today. Sometimes we are made to wonder if God can be heard above all the other noises that surround us in our daily existence.

I like the bumper sticker which says, "My God is not dead, I talked with him this morning." I believe every one of us would agree that God is alive and most of us would say, we can hear the voice of God in a wide variety of ways. But beyond that we need to ask the very pointed question, What's God saying? It's not enough merely to "hear" the voice of God, we need to know what God's saying and the direction in which he's seeking to lead us. If your spiritual apparatus is properly tuned, you can hear the voice of the eternal God as he speaks, as he gives directions, as he seeks to provide strength in weakness, comfort in sorrow, and healing in a time of illness.

I hear the voice of God in the midst of all other voices, and it seems to me he is saying

I Created.

The book of Genesis, written originally in Hebrew, uses a verb translated in the English "create." This verb's meaning is important, for it basically means to bring into being something from nothing. It's a unique verb in the Old Testament, for it is applied to God. Only God can create. God only has the power to bring into being something from nothing.

We use the word *create* carelessly in the English. If we paint a picture, build a building, or make a garment of clothing we're prone to say, "I created this." Actually we took materials already in existence and combined them for the finished product. Not so with God, for God spoke and brought into being from vast nothingness this earth and all of the infinities of the universe.

Scientists are amazed as they extend the limit of their knowledge of the galaxies. It has become increasingly apparent that this earth on which we live is unique. They find nothing else like it out in space. They have not yet found another planet that could support human life, including Mars. They have not found another planet upon which there are living organisms.

Not only did God create this earth, all that's in it and all of the infinities of space, but God also created every human being who has ever lived, who now lives, or who shall live, in individual fashion. God created us, brought us into being, and endowed us with his eternality. We're not made in the image of God insofar as flesh and bones are concerned. We're made in the image of God in that we have something about us that is eternal. From the instant we were born into the world and became living souls, from that instant forevermore, we shall never cease to exist. We are like God in that regard. God made us in his own image. He endowed us with that spark of eternity.

Each of us coming into the world is a distinct creation from the hand of God. No two of us are alike. God has endowed us with an infinite variety of talents, abilities, personality traits, opportunities for service, and capacities. All of us have differing marks. But because God has made us uniquely, because we are made in his image and he has given us precisely those talents and abilities, he desires us to possess. On the basis of that investment, God has a perfect right to expect a return.

What kind of return does God expect on his investment? He expects, of course, a loving response to his commands: simple obedience. He expects a loving concern for other human beings who occupy this world in which we live. He expects loving faithful service in his kingdom's cause. God has made a fantastic investment in us and rightfully expects his investment to pay dividends. He expects something of you because he made you, because he gave you what you have. He has given you the seeing of your eyes, the hearing of your ears, the skill and agility of your hands, the strength of your arms, and the personality you possess to fulfill the responsibility of a job. God expects a return from you. That's not unreasonable, is it? Man was made as the climax of God's creative purpose, bearing his image, and entrusted man with the keeping and dominion over all creation. God assigned us authority over all else.

When we uncover some of the fantastic secrets of nature, God is not taken by surprise. He intended for us to do that. The discovery of the secrets of the atom and nuclear fission was not something which gave God a jolt. Those secrets were there from the beginning. God was waiting for us to develop the ability to unlock them. This entire earth has been given to us to subdue and to be under our dominion.

Our rebellion today comes from the fact that we don't want to be what God created us to be. We don't want to be man, we want to be God. We fall into the selfsame trap into which Adam and Eve fell. God marked out a portion of that bountiful Garden and said, "This is mine. Don't put your greedy hands on that." Adam and Eve decided they knew best. "Who is he to tell us what to do? Happiness lies in doing what God said not to do, so we'll do it. We'll be God." In the same way, you and I are guilty of moral aberrations in the belief that we know best. After all, who is God to forbid us to do anything that we think might possibly be good for us? Pride caused the fall of God's highest creation, both celestial and earthly, for in eternity some of God's holy angels responded to the rebellion of Lucifer and many defected in their pride. Here on earth, man, God's highest creation, rebelled against his authority and power and said, "We'll do it our way."

What is Easter saying to us? Easter is a ringing reaffirmation of the lordship and sovereignty of Jesus Christ! Easter is a reminder that God is God, and we are not God. We don't have the inherent power to come back from the grave alive. We don't have the inherent power to speak and see the response in terms of healing in the life of a sick person, or the giving of sight to a blind person, or the straightening of withered limbs for a lame person. We don't have that power, but God does. He's the sovereign Lord of all creation, including mankind. Having made such a tremendous investment in your life and mine, God has a right to expect a response from a loving, grateful heart.

What is God saying in a world like ours? He's saying I created. He's also saying

I Care.

The fall of man was man's own doing, but God was not willing to give us up. Adam and Eve, our forefathers physically and spiritually, rebelled. They did the same thing you and I do every day. They said, "I'll do it my way." God could have struck them dead. God could have wiped them off the face of the earth and said, "I'll start over." Or God could have said, "In my power I'll force them to obey. I'll point my finger from which a lightning bolt will strike them, and every time they step out of line I'll force them back." He could have elicited response from the heart of man based on tyranny, and we could have lived in cringing fear every day, looking up, fearful that God would pick us out for punishment. But God cared enough for man, though he sinned, to redeem him.

God's caring is wrapped up in a number of historical facts. The first of these is the crucifixion of Jesus Christ on Calvary, revealing how deeply God cares. There's nothing about us that is like God except this spark of eternality, for if we had the majesty, awesome might, and power of God, it's not possible that we would have done what God did to bring man back. In bloodstained garments on a Roman cross, God in human form said to you, to me, and to all mankind, "I love you, and I want you redeemed forever."

Consider another historical fact: Jesus Christ rose from the dead and is alive forevermore. By that resurrection Jesus validated every word he had ever spoken and every deed he'd ever done. Then, after his resurrection, he ascended to be with the Father. There he sits at God's right hand, which is the position of prestige, power, and authority. It is from that vantage point we learn that "He ever liveth to make intercession for them" (Heb. 7:25), yearning for our redemption. God cares.

God cares for us individually and he cares for us as a race, the human race. He cared so much he called a special nation, an obscure, often persecuted nation, and made a covenant with that nation to proclaim his truth. They were given a message to take to the entire world. God indicated to them that in his purpose he would place Israel at the crossroads of the ancient world, and from that spot they could tell all men of his love and concern. Yet just like Christians today, the Jews in ancient times mistook special calling for special privilege and became introverted. They came to believe that the gospel was for them alone. They believed that if others wanted the gospel they first had to become Jews. They broke their covenant with God through disobedience and open rebellion! Their disobedience was expressed in their prejudice toward anyone who was not a Jew.

Then God came in human form as the perfect embodiment of divine love. In Christ, God gained two tremendous victories that blessed the hearts of human beings. On Calvary's cross Jesus Christ won the victory over sin. Sin's power was broken; man, through faith in Christ, is liberated! The other victory was the victory over death. When Christ came forth from the tomb of Joseph of Arimathea, walking again on the face of the earth, alive forevermore, his victory over death was offered to all mankind who would believe in him.

Can you hear the voice of God? He's saying to you and me, "I care." God is as deeply involved in the affairs of men today as he has ever been. On this Easter morning God is saying I created, I care, and

I'm Coming.

Most of us who have been in Sunday School have some familiarity with the interbiblical period. That's the period of years between the writing of the last Old Testament prophecy and the coming of John the Baptist, the forerunner of Jesus Christ. This period of perhaps four hundred years was one of disillusionment, discouragement, and defeat on the part of the Jews. There was no voice from God; there was no prophet to stand and proclaim, "Thus saith the Lord." The Jews looked back on the promises God had made concerning the coming of his Messiah, and perhaps some concluded that "God is dead" or maybe that God was asleep. Many lost hope.

We can look back in the interbiblical period and, though there was no prophet to stand and preach the gospel of God, see the hand of God in the affairs of men.

For instance, it was during the interbiblical period that we discern the rise of the synagogue. Prior to that time true worship was in Jerusalem alone. The people had to go to the Temple in Jerusalem if they were to worship, for there in the holy of holies was to be found the Shekinah presence of God. If one wished to truly worship, he had to go there. The synagogues were smaller representatives of the Temple built in every community where there were faithful followers of God. Synagogues became the forerunner of the Christian church.

Also, during this interbiblical period, there was the unification of the known world under the dominance of the Roman Empire which furnished an ideal platform for the coming of the King and the Christian gospel. Under Roman rule roads were built all over the known world. Roman legionnaires guaranteed the safety and security of people traveling from one place to another. Roman government afforded a system of mail, and all of this contributed to the coming of the King and the preaching of the gospel of Jesus Christ.

Many today cannot discern the hand of God or hear the voice of God. Many then could not. Many then, and some now, thought God was dead. But God was and is at work, nevertheless. In the last twenty-five years we have seen the hand of God moving, perhaps slowly and inexorably but moving, making this world in which we live a neighborhood, though not yet a brotherhood.

The voice of God can be heard in our world speaking in the deepest need of man, prejudice. The problem in the Middle East today, that caldron which if ignited could start a global conflict, is racial prejudice, the hatred of the Jew for the Arab and the Arab for the Jew. The problem in America is a problem of racial prejudice, race against race. The problem in Africa, apartheid, is the same problem of prejudice. It was the problem which caused the Jews to break their covenant with God as they failed to be a saving people and became simply a saved people. So the hand of God moved on, for God was not content with those people and their rebellion.

Arnold Toynbee in his nomothetic approach to history, that is, history based on certain understood laws, has said, "As far as we know human nature has not varied since the earliest date at which our ancestors became recognizably human." What is the basis of history? He said the one unchanging factor in history is human nature. That's the one thing we can see that is truly unchanged. Man is selfish; we are rebellious: we are prejudiced. The one thing about which we can be certain is that human nature has not yet dramatically changed. We are impatient; we tend to discouragement. We ask, Why doesn't God do something; why doesn't God intervene; why doesn't God stop this and stop that? Listen, the Bible tells us that God looks on time in a different way than we do. He sees one year as a thousand and a thousand years as one. Since that's true, it's only been two years, according to God's clock, since Jesus Christ was here on earth.

Most of us have sat through dramatic productions, maybe a play, a musical, or a movie. We have done so as spectators caught up in the emotions and struggles of the characters portrayed. We shared with them so totally that we wept when they wept; we laughed when they laughed; and we felt the pain of defeat or the thrill of victory when they felt it. When the play was over we went our way, somehow aware that what we had seen was fiction. We knew it was intended only for entertainment. We enjoyed a few fleeting moments and then returned to reality, unchanged by what we'd seen and felt. You've had such an experience, so my question is, Do you regard Easter in that light? Is this merely fiction to which we are spectators? When this Easter is over and we reach the end of the day, will we return to a world of stern reality, unchanged by what we have seen and heard and felt? We won't if we correctly understand, for at this Easter season God is saying so very plainly, I created, I care, and I am coming.

It's because Christ is alive that we are able to sing, "Because he lives I can face tomorrow; Because he lives all fear is gone."

4. Quest for Reality

Hebrews 13:8

All of us are familiar with the soft drink advertisement which proclaims its product to be "the real thing." Maybe we've memorized the lyrics, the melody, and hum it throughout the day, often not realizing what we are humming. This is excellent advertisement and subtle motivation. It capitalizes on a basic human drive. Everyone wants the genuine. No one wants a facsimile. Everyone wants an original. No one wants a reproduction. It's the real thing. This advertisement also takes advantage of the restlessness of youth, seeking reality and meaning in life for their existence on earth.

The poet, in a different vein, advised us:

> Life is real! Life is earnest!
> And the grave is not its goal;
> Dust thou art, to dust returneth,
> Was not spoken of the soul.

I wish to extol the truth that reality does not come in bottles, either in liquid or pill form. Reality is not to be found in some hallucinogenic trip nor is it to be found in simply drinking the contents of a soft drink bottle. Reality is not a mirage. It's not something fleeting and passing. Reality is concrete and unchanging.

That is precisely what our text is all about. Our text is about the real One, not the real thing. Jesus Christ alone is impervious to change. Everything else about life and society is changing. Everything about our being changes. As we grow older, some find that hair turns gray; some find it turns loose. Some find that they grow larger; others find they grow smaller. Some of us find our attitude and outlook change dramatically. Our job plans often are radically changed. Frequently we change residences, sometimes within a city and sometimes in an out-of-town move. Our jobs may change. Everything in life changes except one thing. Jesus Christ is the same yesterday, today, and forever. In a world of flux and change he is the one sure foundation. If yours is a quest for reality, I'll point you to him.

Let me remind you of the

Context

in which we are living our lives. We live in a world that literally writhes in confusion and conflict. Our society is marked by hard-line activists, disillusioned idealists, and apathetic permissivists. These are seen in all segments of American life.

Most of us felt that hard-line activists were a thing of the past, then came the Symbionese Liberation Army. We see the disillusioned idealists, for they were that group who thought they could take this nation by force and transform it by violence. But they learned society was too mature for their approach, that the American people would not stand for it. We still see the apathetic permissivists who shrug their shoulders, who possess a "who cares" attitude, who wash their hands of the whole sordid mess, and sit back clucking their tongues in their cheeks as much as to say, "Well, boys will be boys."

In this context we find a great segment of the business world infected with questionable ethics. Some business-men who would never steal a dime have the personal sexual morality of an alley cat. Outstanding civic leaders hold the belief that right and wrong are relative, depend-ing on the one defining right and wrong and what the context is in which the definition is being given. The view that you have a right to anything you want and to anything you can get, as long as it makes you happy, is precisely the morality of Watergate. Morality, integ-rity, and conscience are all painted a nasty gray.

Our avant-garde generation, looking back at some of the abuses and extremes of the past, have rejected and despised Puritan morality, leaving us to exist in an age where persons commit senseless crimes, mindless, point-less atrocities, that many times are imitations of sadistic procedures suggested by television. When a sick mind sees sadism on television, it tries to live it out.

In this context the church is seen as a sinking ship. It's listing badly and water is pouring into the hold. The passengers on the ship are the members of the church and react broadly in three ways. Some apparently try to ignore the whole thing; they keep on playing bridge in the clubroom. They think perhaps it will all go away. Others rush down into the hold to plug up the leaks in the ship and try to bail out and siphon the water to make the ship safe and stable once again. But the third reaction is seen on the part of those who panic. They assume the worst, take to the lifeboats, and try to find safety in leaving the ship. That's a pretty accurate description of our day, for all three categories are found in churches around the world.

The story is told of a professor who was delivering

the final lecture of the semester. He was trying to outline what to expect on the final examination. He was urging the students to devote every moment they could between the end of class and the examination to review the material and to refresh their minds in preparation for the test. He concluded his remarks by saying, "The examination is now in the hands of the secretary to be mimeographed." Before dismissing the class, he asked, "Are there any questions?" Silence prevailed. Finally a voice from the rear asked, "Who's the secretary?"

Ours is the age of the rip-off, the cop-out, the fast buck, the goof-off, and all the rest. That's the kind of world in which we live, but the morality of others is simply a reflection of our own morality. The same individuals who will cheat on an examination someday will be involved in Watergate-type offenses. The same ones who take the moral shortcuts early in life will be the ones who will try to corner the market unfairly and garner windfall profits. They will be the ones to elbow anyone who gets in their way as they advance their own cause. So the seeds of disillusionment, the seeds of sin, can be seen in the lives of young people while the harvest is in view in the lives of older persons.

In that kind of context, what are the

Choices

that face us? Probably the most prominent choice now is hedonism. That's a big word which merely means to live by the pleasure principle, to live your life for selfish gratification.

There are two basic principles bidding for the allegiance of men. One is the pleasure principle, and at the opposite end of the spectrum is the reality principle.

The pleasure principle says, "I don't know what's going to happen tomorrow. I'm going to get all I can today. I'm going to leave no door closed, no stone unturned, the here and now is it." For those in quest for reality, the reality principle suggests that, "because of what tomorrow holds, I'll act this way today." Because of the challenges of the world in which I live, I'll make preparation today for those challenges and try to be ready to do whatever God wants me to do. I'll try to prepare my mind, prepare my spirit, prepare and keep my body strong and healthy, and not do those things that will abuse and desecrate this temple of the Holy Spirit. I'll not fill my life with commitment to things temporal and fleeting, but I'll give myself to those things that are immutable and shall never die.

The hedonist philosophy is summed up in a bumper sticker I have seen. It says, "If it feels good, do it." That's the philosophy by which millions of Americans are living. These shallow, superficial, pleasure-crazed individuals play hopscotch with the commandments of Almighty God and think that life consists in doing anything they like to do. All the while, with arrogance and ignorance, they try to relativize the standard by which God one day will judge all men and nations. We ought not be surprised at this, however. The Bible clearly tells us that in the last days men are going to be "lovers of pleasure more than lovers of God." (2 Tim. 3:4). I'm sure there has never been a day in which that was more true than now.

Another of the choices that faces us in our quest for reality is humanism. This is the view widely held in our world that pictures man as the ultimate. "I am the master of my fate, I am the captain of my soul." This philosophy

rejects the supernatural. It destroys any sense of need
for God, for worship, for fellowship in the faith, or for
the belief in anything which cannot be explained by the
rational powers of the mind of man.

In our time, the outstanding monument to humanism
is Hitler's Third Reich. It was based on such an atheistic
philosophy. Forty-seven percent of his S.S. troops, his
elite soldiers, held postgraduate degrees. That humanistic philosophy so permeated Germany, at least those
in leadership, that the nation which produced men like
Bach, Beethoven, and Wagner also produced Dachau,
Auschwitz, and Buchenwald.

F. H. Littell, chairman of the National Conference
of Christians and Jews, observed that Auschwitz was a
hell on earth produced by a perfect science, planned
by professors, and built by Ph.D.'s. And then he went
on to state, to our chagrin, that what was done in those
places was carried out by baptized church members.
That's the ultimate in humanistic philosophy: a complete
disregard for the value of human personality, for the
sanctity of man made in the image of God, and the exal-
tation of any individual who is able to achieve power
by his own initiative.

Many choices face us today, but another possible
choice centers in the person of Jesus Christ. I cannot
speak with objectivity concerning this choice. I'm subjec-
tive here, for it happens that I know Jesus Christ as
my personal Savior. I do not present the case for Christianity; I'm not about to discuss church membership. I
desire to present Jesus Christ, the Son of God. With
all the criticism that may be directed toward his church
or his followers, there has never been a voice in history
raised to denounce Jesus. There was never a voice raised

in his own day, either by religious leaders or pagans, to denounce the life-style of Jesus Christ or accuse him of any sin. Never in history's annals has anyone ever been able to disparage the Son of God, Jesus Christ. He stands today unchanged, the same yesterday, today, and forever.

Admittedly, some of his followers are hypocrites, and before you say others are hypocrites, I would ask you to confront yourself with the question: Am I a hypocrite? If you are honest you'll say, 'Yes, I am! I have never, nor do I now, lived up to my highest idealism."

I talk frequently with people who are at least infidels and possibly atheistic, but I have never found a one who in any honest self-confrontation would state that he was living up to his highest ideals, whatever they were.

Who is the hypocrite? The hypocrite is one who knows what he ought to do and doesn't do it, the one who tries to playact, who lives his life behind a mask trying to make you believe he's something he isn't. Yes, there are hypocrites among us, and I'm one of them and so are you!

This church is not perfect; it is not now, it has never been, nor will it ever be. Perfection is reserved for that blissful moment when we will stand in the presence of our Lord, clothed in the beauty of a resurrection body, living without sin in the presence of our Redeemer through all eternity. Yes, there are hypocrites in the church. My answer to those critics who point this out so ferociously is, come on in, the water's fine! There are hypocrites out there, too, in any direction you might look.

Others criticize by saying Christ's churches are cold

and dead, insensitive and speechless in any age of dire need. That's true also in part, but I can guarantee that's not true of some churches I know. Though marked by sin, inconsistency, and failure, many are seeking daily to faithfully proclaim the gospel of Jesus Christ.

Sometimes people leave the fellowship of a church for another fellowship, but it's not because the church is irrelevant. In most cases it's because the relevancy of the proclamation of the gospel causes such discomfort that one can't stand it. Rather than stay in the kitchen where the heat is intense, they move out. Yes, there are cold, dead churches. Probably you know some, but there are a lot of other churches that are so relevant and so direct with the proclamation of the gospel that people find it just doesn't fit their life-style. Unwilling to make the sacrifice Jesus Christ commands and directs, they turn their backs and go in the other direction. Disobedience to God soon leads to defiance of God.

Many choices face us today, but in the midst of these choices I want to tell you of my

Confidence

in Jesus Christ. Without apology or equivocation I remind you that if every person in America would receive Jesus Christ in the fullness of regeneration and sanctification, it would solve each problem facing our nation. If you want to make a contribution to society, to do something that will be lasting, to perpetuate the ideals of America, there is no way in which that can be done more effectively than through an effort to evangelize this nation and bring the lost to know Jesus Christ.

If all Americans were born again, there would be no serious problems left. It would solve every home problem. If every husband loved his wife deeply enough to die for her, if every wife loved her husband deeply enough to die for him, divorce lawyers would have to find employment elsewhere.

Conversion to Jesus Christ would solve the war problem by sundown, for if each person loved every other person well enough to lay down his life for him, he would not kill. There would be no bloodshed and no atomic holocaust.

The problems of capital and labor would immediately be solved if everyone were Christians. If every employer loved his employees well enough to die for them, if every employee loved his employer well enough to die for him, then there would be no strikes, no starvation wages, no unfair advantage taken of any other human being.

If all of us were truly born again, there would be no conflicts between races. If all white people were Christians and loved all the Christian black people enough to die for them and the black people loved the white people that way, all of our racial problems would disappear. If we loved every other nationality on the face of the earth like that, there would be no problems of prejudice.

If every one of us loved every other one enough to die for him, there wouldn't be any secrets, there wouldn't be any need for wiretaps, bugging, payoffs, hush money, lies and more lies to cover up lies, threats, abuses of authority, and every other problem you find in the world of politics. If we loved each other enough to die for one another, the problems would be non-existent.

What's the answer? The answer is let our politicians

crown Christ as Lord, and the solutions will come. Let
our schools crown Christ as Lord, and learning then
will have its source in one who is the truth and is the
same yesterday, today, and forever. Let businessmen
crown Christ as Lord, and commerce will assume its
rightful and honorable place in society. Let the home
crown Christ as Lord and the home will be a little vesti-
bule to heaven.

Jesus Christ, the one whom I have come to extol today,
still possesses drawing power. When you find a church
where men are not being drawn to Christ, it's not
Christ's fault; it's because Christ has not been lifted up.
When he's lifted up, he will draw all men unto himself!
He's only lifted up when crucified churches reveal a crucified Christ through a sanctified ministry and a regener-
ated church membership. If you are in a quest for reality,
if you are looking for the real thing, I'm pointing you
to Jesus, God's Son with power and the Son of man
without sin. He is the one who is real and genuine,
no superficial facsimile, but the same yesterday, today,
and forever.

Particularly for this graduating class, I'd like to point
to Jesus; whatever else in this world may change in the
days to come, he is unchanging. He is the God of our
fathers, the God of Abraham, Isaac, and Jacob. He was
the God of our forefathers who came to this land. He
laid the foundation upon which we are building. He is
still a God of mercy, the same yesterday, today, and
forever.

5. Wedlock or Deadlock?

Ephesians 5:33

Scientists suggest atoms are the building blocks of the universe. In that same sense we can say homes are the building blocks of the social order. Jesus Christ is the world's greatest home builder. That immediately clarifies something for a Christian. It implies that Satan, who is antithetical to Jesus Christ, is the world's greatest home wrecker. When you find a home on the rocks, you don't see the purpose of God revealed, but the purpose of Satan. It's Satan's purpose to tear down, to wreck, and to destroy everything God builds up, constructs, and seeks to make useful.

It is under satanic influence that marriages move from wedlock to deadlock, or put in another way, from altar to altercation, perhaps from bliss to bombast, from contentment to conflict, or maybe from a duet to a duel. God's purpose is to strengthen and build the home. Satan's purpose is to weaken and destroy this building block in the social order.

No one can properly understand or appreciate marriage apart from the intention of God. Speaking from the Christian perspective I'd like to point you to the

Place

of the home.

In God's plan for the human race we are to have three homes. We have a family home, that is, an earthly home, a church home, and a heavenly home. God's design is for Jesus Christ to be Lord of all three. He is not Lord indeed unless he is Lord of all: Lord of our family home, Lord in our church home, and Lord in our heavenly or eternal home.

Going back to the beginning of the human race, in that blissful bower of perfection, the Garden of Eden, God united the first man and the first woman in marriage and blessed their relationship. Marriage was not begun for the propagation of the human race or merely for convenience. Marriage was instituted for the happiness and well-being of mankind. God said: "It is not good that the man should be alone; I will make him an help meet for him" (Gen. 2:18). In that one statement God pointed out that life lived in isolation is never complete. Man was not intended to live in seclusion or separated from others. Life was designed to be shared and given in the most intimate of all relationships, that of marriage. God designed marriage to be a duet and not a solo. It's the union of one man and one woman in bonds severed only by death. Marriage is to be a partnership and not a veritable tug-of-war.

The place of the home is one of priority, for the home established in marriage is to assume ascendency over every other home on earth. Your home is more important than any other home and that includes your parental home. A proper understanding of the place of the home would eliminate many modern problems related to family living.

If the home occupies its rightful place, there must be an understanding of the places within the home.

There is first the place of the husband. Writing in Colossians 3:18 the apostle Paul stated, "Wives, submit yourselves unto your own husbands, as it is fit in the Lord." The word "submit" does not mean knuckle under to, nor does it picture a kind of slavery. The word in this context means to put the other person in the place of rank or honor. That's precisely the place God has given to the husband and father in the home, a place of rank or honor. Without equivocation it can be flatly stated that one is outside the will of God to marry a man who cannot be respected and to whom tribute cannot be paid. It's God's plan for wives to reverence and honor their husbands. That's not to imply dictatorship or tyranny, but it is to honor and recognize strong spiritual leadership. That's the place of the father.

If one is married to a man who has no interest in a study of the Bible, God's road map for life, or one who has no interest in the church, which is Christ's holy bride and body, if the husband has no interest in spiritual things, there will be serious problems. It's God's will for a wife to reverence, honor, and pay tribute to her husband, the father of her children, the man whom she has married.

But that's not the whole story. There are other places in the home. There is also the place of the wife. Paul pointed out that wives are to be offered the highest love conceivable. In Ephesians 5:25, under inspiration of the Holy Spirit, Paul wrote: "Husbands, love your wives even as Christ also loved the church." That's the responsibility of the husband, to love his wife in the same way Christ loved the church.

Do you think Christ would take an unfair advantage of his church? Do you think he'd pull a dirty trick on

the church? Do you think he'd try to maneuver the
church into such a spot that he could get it under his
heel and grind it down? Do you think that he would
slip up on the blind side of his church and take some
cheap shot at it? Not on your life! A husband is to love,
honor, respect, and cherish his wife in the same way
Christ does the church.

This is not a matter of one partner in marriage assum-
ing ascendency over the other. It's a matter of partnership, for each has a place in the eternal purpose of God.
The wife is to be given the same kind of respect, reverence, and honor as the husband.

Dr. G. Campbell Morgan, who was one of the great
Bible expositors of a past generation, had four sons,
all of whom were preachers. One day at a family gathering someone walked into the drawing room where all
were present. Trying to find out what one of the sons,
Howard, was made of, this person asked, "Howard, who
is the greatest preacher in your family?" Howard had
the highest admiration for his father and looked straight
across the room at him, but without a moment's hesita-
tion replied, "Mother."

Mothers, you see, play an indispensable role in the
home, and the philosophy of the mother is all-important.
It makes a great deal of difference whether a mother
and wife conceives of homemaking and all it involves
as life's highest calling. If she does, the chances are
she has a scriptural, healthy home which is a strong
force for good in society. But if she feels homemaking
and being a mother and housewife is demeaning, an
unhealthy situation develops and the home detracts from
society rather than contributing to it.

In any home under God, there is also a place for

the children. These are the three places within the home: the husband and father, the wife and mother, and the children. The children can contribute to the success of a home. That's the reason Paul wrote, "Children, obey your parents in all things: for this is well pleasing unto the Lord" (Col. 3:20).

There are many in the younger generation who reject the word *obedience*, who don't want to obey or submit to any other human being. But regardless of that segment of youth in America, this is God's command: "Children, obey your parents."

Let's pause for a word to the parents. When parents fail to teach their children to obey, they are cruel and counterproductive. Jesus Christ obeyed his earthly parents; if we are his followers, we can do no less. Young people today cannot be evaluated in their Christian witness solely on the basis of the words they speak, for many of them know the right words. They have the correct vocabulary. They can talk with great glibness about Jesus. But the thing that speaks louder than their words is the life-style they have adopted in relation to their parents. "Children, obey your parents," for this is right. This is the way you prove you are honoring the Lord.

There comes a time when a child is no longer a child. Children grow up, and there is a time when decisions have to be made on the part of growing young persons. But the tragic truth is if a child is not taught obedience in the home, he becomes a counterproductive citizen in society, for he will also ignore the laws of the land. He'll show disrespect for those who enforce the law and try to tear down and destroy, through anarchy, that which has been created and built up by law and order.

Many of the problems on college campuses and in

various communities across our nation in the last decade have come, in the main, from young people who were not taught obedience in their homes. Permissive parents simply let their children do anything, anytime, without parental requirements or expectations established within the home. There is a place for the husband and father, the wife and mother, a place for the children, and all of these are under God.

Now a word about God's

Provision

for the home.

To understand marriage we must understand man. Man is threefold: body, mind, and spirit. We're created after the likeness of God, and God is triune: Father, Son, and Spirit. Man's body is his physical nature, related to the world beneath him. Man's mind is his psychological or intellectual nature, and it's related to life around and about him. Man's spirit is his soul and is related to life above and beyond him. In the purpose of God, normal life physically leads to health. Normal life psychologically leads to happiness. Normal life spiritually leads to holiness. One must understand the nature of man to understand marriage and the investment of all three areas, if he's to live a normal, happy life.

In marriage two persons become one flesh, one in body, one in mind, and one in spirit. If you have a healthy marriage this has to do with the physical, in which sex becomes the highest expression of love and oneness of which two humans are capable. It is the most intimate of all human experiences. A healthy marriage is one in which there is a good sexual relationship.

A happy marriage is one in which two persons become

one psychologically. They have the same outlook and attitude toward life, life-styles, society around them, and on what constitutes true happiness.

A holy marriage is one in which two persons are spiritually united. Jesus Christ becomes the center and circumference of their existence.

What's the matter with the home today? Why the spiraling divorce rate? Why is home life disintegrating? It's because there are millions of homes that have one-third of a marriage. It's based on the physical, on sex, and that's mere lust, not love. When people only have one-third of a marriage, they can never find fulfillment and happiness.

There are many homes that have two-thirds of a marriage. They have the physical relationship and psychological unity. There are a lot of young people who are physically attracted and have a lot in common. They have a Volkswagen van and long hair; they have the same life-styles. Psychologically and physically they possess two-thirds of a marriage. They often wonder why, after a brief period of time, they became disenchanted with each other and head for a divorce court, if they ever went to the trouble to get married. What's the problem? The problem is they didn't start with a marriage. They had a fraction of a marriage, a portion of a marriage. That which they had was not God's provision; it was not the fulfillment of God's plan.

A home is divine in establishment. God planned it. If you marry outside the will of God and with a faulty understanding of man, there's not much chance for you to have a happy, lasting home. Marriage is supreme in its relationships. Let it be stated as dogmatically as possible that your home, in the plan of God, is to come ahead of your business, ahead of your in-laws, ahead of your pleasure, or any mundane matter! If it doesn't, your home is in trouble.

I can recall home after home on the rocks because the husband has put business ahead of his family. I can name many other homes on the rocks because one or the other of the marriage partners put in-laws ahead of the other and home. That's not the way God intended it to be. The home is supreme in relationships. Next to your vertical relationship to God comes your horizontal responsibility to your family. When you put any thing ahead of either one of those, you have stepped out of the purpose of God. Let me remind you of the

Permanence

of the home.

The home is unconditional in commitment, for it is until death do you two part. What is marriage in your judgment, till death or till differences? What are you to do when moonlight and roses becomes daylight and diapers? When you are up to your elbows in dishwater? When you are covered up with the monthly bills? What are you to do when that time comes?

The same God who requires premarital chastity requires post-marital fidelity. That's fidelity in body, mind, and spirit: physically, psychologically, and spiritually. If you haven't got that kind of home, you may have rushed into marriage.

For the benefit of the single adults, there are a lot of things worse than staying single. Don't ever let anyone push you into marriage. One of the things worse than staying single is to marry the wrong person.

Gladys Keith, a noble home missionary who began

much of the home mission work we have in the city of New Orleans, Louisiana, was one of God's unclaimed blessings. She use to laugh when people asked her why she never married. She replied, "Because it's scriptural." Then they'd ask her what she meant. She'd reply, "Well, my favorite verse of Scripture is the one that says, 'I would not have you ignorant, brethren'" (Rom. 1:13). So, if you ladies are single, you can use that verse of Scripture and stay that way!

For those of you who have had tragic marriages and unfortunate divorces, you can't go back. I'm not condemning you, but there is something you can do now. You can't unscramble eggs, but you can commit your present home to God and make what you have now a true marriage.

The home which has permanence is based on the concept of Christian marriage, and Christian marriage means one man and one woman until death.

About 75 percent of the young people who ask me to perform their marriage ceremonies, and come for the counseling sessions, have no concept of the permanence of marriage. They are in a different world, a different ball park. They have somehow concluded that marriage is a ninety-day arrangement or a matter of convenience, or a trial and error proposition. They've never understood that in the purpose of God marriage is permanent! For life! One man, one woman, and the two become one flesh; body, mind, and spirit.

As bad as the divorce statistics sound, we need to give the positive emphasis. Approximately two-thirds of the people who get married in America live with the person they marry until one of them dies. It's true that one-third, or maybe one-fourth to one-third of those who marry, have marriages that go on the rocks. It's hard to know in that one-fourth to one-third how many are repeaters. The repeaters are the ones who have problems; they usually make the same mistake two or three times. They rush into marriage again and don't stop to think. They find themselves continually in hot water.

There are many things in life that change. Your job may change. Your residence may change. Your friends may change. Your health may change. Your status in life, your fortune may change, but marriage is permanent! It's permanent when it's based on moral security, when a man can trust his wife to behave when he's away and has a wife who can be trusted. It's based on a wife who knows her husband is going to be true to his marriage vows even when he's in a distant city attending a convention. That's moral security.

A permanent home is also based on emotional security. A person needs to know he is accepted at home regardless of his shortcomings, his foibles, frailties, and faults. To know there is a place where he is accepted, even if he is a failure, is emotional security.

Marriage is a permanent relationship when based on understanding, communication, and the same kind of love that God has for you and me. A God kind of love loves even when the object is unlovely. We may not be lovable all the time, but in a Christian home, there is a continuing love based not on human likes and dislikes. This love is based on the same kind of love God had in Christ when he loved us and redeemed us. What's your home, wedlock or deadlock?

6. The High Road
Acts 20:35

The poet John Oxenham wrote the following lines.

> To every man there openeth
> A Way, and Ways, and a Way,
> And the High Soul climbs the High Way,
> And the Low Soul gropes the Low;
> And in between, on the misty flats,
> The rest drift to and fro.
> But to every man there openeth
> A High Way and a Low,
> And every man decideth
> The Way his soul shall go.

There's no arena of life in which this is more applicable than in the matter of Christian stewardship. Every man decideth. We've heard many marvelous personal testimonies from Christians who have spoken from the voice of experience. It has been said in various ways that Christian stewardship is nothing more or less than the economic result of a spiritual experience. I believe that is true. The deeper the experience, the greater one's sense of Christian stewardship.

The belief that man owns, rather than God, is a pagan concept, not a Christian belief. The Christian has faith in the fact that "The earth is the Lord's, and the fullness thereof; the world, and they that dwell therein" (Ps. 24:1). Stewardship and service for the Christian are but the rent we pay for the space we occupy on the face of God's earth. The high road of life is the road of Christian stewardship.

To support that contention I'd like to begin by relating some

Facts

about stewardship. We'll also talk about faith; and finally, we'll refer to the future.

Our text states a fact. It is a fact because it comes from the lips of Jesus Christ, the omniscient Son of God. With all knowledge, knowing every one of us, Jesus said, "It is more blessed to give than to receive" (Acts 20:35). Most of us, unfortunately, feel like the cynic who said, "It may be more blessed to give than receive, but receiving's good enough for me." Most of us prefer to receive than to give. Yet Jesus said it's more blessed to give.

Now is that mere idealism? Is there any substance to a statement like that? Is this a fact? Keep in mind that we learned in Vacation Bible School days that the Greek word translated "blessed" is better translated "happy." Happy. Jesus really said it's happier to give than to receive. Have you ever learned that joy? have you found that happiness?

Honestly now, which had you rather be, a beggar or a benefactor? patient or physician? an asset or a liability? a blessing or a blight? a giver or a getter? part of the problem or part of the solution? Our text is not just idealistic prattle. Our text is the wisdom of God and the voice of eternity. It is happier to give than to receive. Jesus proves this. He is our authority. He came into this world, not to receive but to empty himself. He came not to get, but to give. He came with no thought of personal gain. The only reward he received was a cross and the joy of fulfilling God's eternal redemptive purpose.

One very generous, faithful Christian steward was asked the secret of the blessedness he displayed in life. His answer was, "I've discovered that God has a bigger shovel than I have. God can shovel it in a whole lot faster than I can shovel it out."

Those are not the only facts in the case. It is a fact that the giver has a clear conscience toward God. The getter, by contrast, is the unhappiest person on the face of the earth. No matter how much he gets, he always wants more. Have you had that happen? Have you experienced this? You have already received everything you ever dreamed of getting from the standpoint of what the world has to offer. Nonetheless, you are unhappy; you want more.

Those of us who grew up in depression days never in our wildest dreams thought we would have what we have today. But are our hearts content? Have we learned to be happy in whatever state we find ourselves? Not at all. We still are gripped by the sin of covetousness. No matter how much we have, we still want more. That sin has marred our fellowship with God. Such a person is unhappy when he is not giving because he was made in the image of God. Man was made to be a channel, not a reservoir. When your purpose in life is to hoard, to save, and to get, to be able to add it up and look at it and count it and measure it, that purpose is self-defeating. It is contrary to the purpose of the God who made you, who saved you, and who put you in this earth to be a Christian steward.

This inner unhappiness or discontent makes a person

a disgruntled, critical church member. These are the ones who get mad when asked to give or pledge. When they separate themselves from a dollar, they begin to sing their well-known theme song, "When we asunder part, It gives us inward pain," and it does! It gives many persons inward pain to separate themselves from a dollar. But this is not so for the Christian steward who has found the secret of life and Christian living in the words of Jesus, "It's happier to give than to receive."

When we live our lives like sponges, soaking up everything around us and giving nothing, we automatically create an atmosphere and aura of misery and spiritual discontent. It's inevitable, for such a life-style is in total opposition to God's plan and purpose for us.

These are some of the facts of the case, but let me remind you of the

Faith

required of a Christian if he's to become a Christian steward. Where faith in God is strong, Christian stewardship abounds. But the reverse side of that coin is just as true. Where faith in God is anemic, Christian stewardship diminishes proportionately.

When God gets all of a man, he gets his property. Does God have all of you? When Jesus got Simon Peter, he got his boat. The day came when Jesus needed a boat in which to stand and push back from the shore to address tens of thousands of people. He had a boat that day because he had the boat's owner.

Does Jesus have a house at your address? Does Jesus have a business in the place where you have an office? Does Jesus have an automobile because you have an automobile? Does Jesus have leisuretime because you have leisuretime? Does Jesus have a day off when you have a day off? When God gets a man in totality, he gets all the man has. When he gets a man of wealth, Jesus has wealth for the kingdom of God. But if a man says he belongs to Jesus but holds on to his possessions, he has denied his profession.

Jesus doesn't want us in bits and pieces, cut up and divided and separated one part from the other. He doesn't just want your emotions; he wants your mind. He doesn't just want your hands; he wants your eyes. He doesn't just want your time; he wants your treasure. He wants all you have and are, and that's what it means to be a Christian!

When Christ is Lord, we're stewards. Change the word *Lord* to *boss.* It seems to mean more to some people. Jesus is Boss. That means when Jesus says, "I want this done," we say, "Yes, sir, Boss, that's what is going to be done."

Now if we argue about it, Jesus isn't Lord. He isn't Boss at all. We stand around and whine, "I don't want to do that. That's not my cup of tea. That's not my bag. Somebody else . . . ." Jesus isn't Lord in that life. The high road of Christian stewardship is the road of faith, not sight. It is not doing just what we see can be accomplished, but doing what we can accomplish with the resources of heaven and in the power of God!

How do you express this kind of faith? Let's say you are a growing Christian and interested. You are saying in your heart, "Preacher, tell me what I must do." I'm not going to tell you what you must do, but I will tell you some things God's Word says we must do. I believe God's Word tells us that we have to give up to God in the matter of our personal finances.

Some of you have been in financial trouble ever since you got on your own. I've got news for you! You are going to stay in financial hot water until you turn your finances over to God.

Two lumberjacks decided to paddle across the lake to a tavern on Saturday night. They paddled their canoe all the way across the huge lake, tied it at the shore, and went up to the tavern. Before the evening was spent they got roaring drunk. They eventually made their way back to the canoe and were going to row across the lake and go back to camp. They got in the boat and paddled and paddled and paddled until they were exhausted. They looked around and discerned, to their dismay, that they had never even gotten away from the shore. They were exhausted, no strength left, so they fell asleep in the boat. When they were awakened the next morning by the rising sun, they discovered the problem. They had never untied the boat from the dock. Now that's like a couple of drunks, isn't it? Typical. Just as typical as finding beer cans littering the streets and highways. That's typical of beer drinkers. That's what you expect of their mentality. Well, you expect a bunch of drunks not to untie the boat and try to paddle across the lake with the boat still tied.

But that does not apply just to those who are inebriated. I know thousands of Christians who have fought the battle of the budget and lost. They just can't make ends meet. There is too much month left over when the money runs out. You wonder why in the world you can't keep your head above water financially? I'll tell you why. You haven't untied the canoe! You've never turned your personal finances over to God under the lordship of Christ. You begin that when you give him his part. That top tenth belongs to him.

Somebody says, "But I'm in debt." Sure you are, but for what are you in debt? You are in debt for those things you wanted personally and selfishly and you bought them, even though it obligated you up to your ears. You may *want* a lot of things you don't *need*. God never said he'd supply all your wants, but the Bible teaches, and I believe, that God will supply your needs according to his riches in glory through Jesus Christ! You may not have needed a new car. You've got to make the payments on it, and there isn't any money left when you get through making the payments. You built that big new home and moved into it, and you're obligated so you can't do anything else financially. Is that God's fault? No, that's your own selfishness. Don't blame God for it. Your greatest debt, the biggest debt you owe is your debt to God, who gives you life and health and strength.

To whom do you owe your greatest debt? You owe it to the one who gives you life, health, and strength, and until you are ready to acknowledge that, you're not ready to do business for God, with God, or let him do business through you.

Others say, "Well, I don't know what I make." That's an interesting statement. Tell that to the Internal Revenue; maybe they'll help you figure out what you make. If they believe you, maybe God would also. I think you know how ridiculous that is.

Let me urge you to have faith enough in God to give an honest tithe. And by that I mean every paycheck you receive, every bonus, every commission, every dollar of income that you get, give an honest tithe. Tithe it all. Give a full tithe. Don't start trying to decide what all you may deduct, for these deductions soon become self-defeating. If you are not very careful, you'll end up statistically with God owing you. Don't try to scheme and figure loopholes like you do when you figure your 1040.

Now I know that it's possible in the United States of America for a wealthy businessman to go year after year without paying any income tax at all. In fact, in a recent year I read where the former governor of New York, who is a member of one of the wealthiest families America has ever had, voluntarily gave to the United States government some ten thousand dollars, though he really was not obligated to pay income tax under our laws.

You may get by with that as far as the law is concerned and our government, but friend, I don't believe there is a person on the face of the earth who is not in debt to God. You may be able to deduct all your income businesswise, but you are in debt to God and are not exonerated from any obligation to God financially just because the laws of the land might exempt you from the payment of income tax.

Give the true tithe. That means bring 10 percent of your income into the storehouse, which is the local church. Figure on your home. You say, "Well, I don't pay the tithe on the part that I am paying on my house." Yes, when you get through your house payments, you'll own your home and have a twenty, twenty-five, or fifty thousand dollar asset there for which you paid not one dime in tithe money. If your business furnishes you with an automobile, that's an asset. I personally feel an obligation to tithe on an estimated amount of how much that means to me in a month's time. Give an honest tithe. Give a full tithe, and do it out of three motives:

Love for Jesus Christ, obedience to Jesus Christ, and service in Jesus Christ.

There's one other word about stewardship,

Future.

I remember well my first pastorate. I entered the New Orleans seminary in September 1948, and in October I was called to a country church with half-time preaching, in Pike County, Mississippi. It was five miles out of Magnolia; friend, when you get to Magnolia, you're "out there" pretty far. Go five miles farther out than Magnolia, and you are way out there! At the end of my first year as pastor, business was booming in that little half-time church. They were paying me the magnificent sum of twenty-five dollars a Sunday, fifty dollars a month.

I didn't know it, but that church was accustomed to extending an annual call. On my first anniversary the chairman of the deacons stood and said, "Preacher, we'd like for you to step outside for a moment." That wasn't hard to do because that Baptist church and its builders had great wisdom and provided a door right behind the pulpit which led to the outside. It was used for many purposes by many preachers! But it was handy, and they asked me to step out, so I did. After a few minutes the chairman of the deacons, "Uncle Dud" Simmons, came to the door and said, "Come on back in, Preacher." I went back in while he announced with great dignity that they had just voted to extend me another annual call. I thanked them and asked them all to sit down. Then I said, "Now, I've got a word. Before I give you my answer as to whether I'm going to accept, I want to ask for two things from you. I want you first to vote to go full time and have preaching every Sunday. Secondly, I want you to extend me an indefinite call, so according to the leadership of God I may stay here as long as I feel it's right, or until the church feels that I should move." Everything got quiet and then Uncle Dud said, "Well, we'll need to vote on this. Would you step outside?" I went outside again. I was gone a little longer that time, but when I finally was invited to come back Uncle Dud stated, "Preacher, we voted to extend you an indefinite call." I thanked him and I asked, "What about the other matter?" He replied, "We want you to moderate the meeting." I answered, "Fine, I'll be glad to." Then I opened the floor for a motion or for discussion.

In the back of the church stood one of the deacons. He'd been a deacon in that church for forty years and never strained a trace, but he'd worn out forty backing straps. Now some of you know what I'm talking about. That deacon stood and with great solemnity said, "Brother Pastor, I move that this church begin a full time program and we double your salary, paying you twenty-five dollars every Sunday instead of twenty-five dollars every other Sunday." Well, the motion was made, it was seconded, and duly passed. The man who made the motion had not given fifty cents to that church in forty years.

Boy, we are big on spending other folk's money, aren't we? That's easy for us to do. The future of a church with that kind of leader is not very bright. But I'm convinced that the future of New Testament churches is gloriously bright, because the spiritual leaders are people who put up and don't shut up. The future of any church will remain bright as long as men and women committed to God's plan of finance are elected to places of leadership and spiritual responsibility.

No born-again believer is too poor to tithe. There may be some who think they are too rich to tithe. There may be some who ought to pray that God will make them poor enough so they can be honest with him. Have you ever prayed that prayer? If you think you've got too much money to be honest with God and tithe, ask God to reduce your income to the point that you can be honest with him. Maybe God will answer that prayer. Maybe you'll get back down on your knees before God, realizing upon whom you are dependent.

The tithe is the Lord's, not ours. It's his. It was established under law and validated under grace. Jesus didn't abolish the law. He said, "I am not come to destroy, but to fulfill" (Matt. 5:17). What was begun under law is even a greater obligation to those of us who are under grace.

The word *tithe* means 10 percent. Where is it to be given? Strangely enough there is a great deal of confusion about this. Seven times in the New Testament the disciples are said to have been gathered on the first day of the week for worship. Five of those seven times the Lord himself honored the assembly by appearing and worshiping with them. Our Lord ordained the gathering and made the first day of the week special by rising from the dead on Sunday morning. The clearly established percentage is 10 percent, and it's to be brought to the weekly gathered assembly.

Now you ask, "What is that assembly?" It's the New Testament church. Jesus, the Lord of the church, has charged the church with the responsibility of making disciples, baptizing them, and teaching them to observe all the other things Christ commanded us.

The word *church* in the New Testament is found 119 times. That Greek word refers, more than 90 percent of the time, to the local body of baptized believers. Only a handful of times does it refer to the church at large, the church composed of all believers everywhere. Actually, that church has not yet been assembled, and it will not be assembled until the last unbeliever God foreordained to be saved has been saved and Jesus returns to this earth.

Where are Christians to give God's tithe? They are to bring that 10 percent into the body of baptized believers who meet on the Lord's Day to do the Lord's work in all of the Lord's earth. That's the high road of Christian stewardship. Let us then walk that road for the honor of our Lord.

> To every man there openeth
> A High Way and a Low,
> And every man decideth
> The Way his soul shall go.

It's up to you.

7. Head of the House

Ephesians 5:22–23

Several years ago a friend who formerly lived in our city, a deacon in the church, called me late one night. I recognized his voice when I answered, and he asked, "Who wears the pants in your family?" Now you don't have any difficulty imagining what my answer was, but I ought to have known that it was a trap. Just as soon as I boldly asserted who the head of our house was he said, "Now if you really run that show, then you're going to be ready in the morning at 3:00 A.M. and go fishing with me." My role in the home had been questioned, and I had boldly asserted myself, so I had no alternative but to go. It was another one of those useless days, and though I did as much good as he did, neither of us caught but one fish apiece. I spent the day down at Lake Graham paddling around in an inner tube, throwing a plug, and then reeling it in. And all to prove I was the head of the house.

On this Father's Day, though it's not a religious observance, I want to refresh your memory with some biblical advice found in our text. According to God's eternal, divine plan the husband is to be the head of the house. I make no apology for that statement even in a day of woman's lib. The Bible is the Word of God. I accept it as such and make no apology for it; I simply proclaim it according my understanding.

In any home where a father abdicates his role as head of the house chaos will result. It may be chaos in the parent-child relationship; it may be chaos in the child-to-child relationship or in the parent-parent relations. There is inevitable trouble when a father fails to assume his position as the head of the house.

We tend to focus the blame for the failure of the home on working mothers, preoccupied or ineffective wives, or maybe society-minded females. All of these may bear a part of the responsibility, but let's focus our attention upon the father and his responsibility in the home.

You know that the home was the first institution of the Old Testament while the church is the first institution of the New Testament. There is no conflict between these two. When one is in right relationship with God through Jesus Christ, the home and the church are not enemies one of the other and neither excludes the other. They are mutually self-supportive. That is God's divine plan, and it is in that vein that I want to point to the father, the head of the house, in his relationship to his

Wife.

The sign on a bulletin board brought to mind a very important truth. It read, "The most important thing a father can do for his children is to love their mother." The most important thing that you, as the head of the house, can do for your family is to love your wife the mother of your children. That provides security in the home that can be gained in no other way. Blessed and happy are the children whose parents truly love each other, for children can tell a phony a mile away. Children know long before parents announce it or file for divorce in court that there's no love between husband and wife, the father and mother.

Some women fear to give themselves to the admonition of our text, "Wives, submit yourselves unto your own husbands" (Eph. 5:22). That fear is based on the possibility of being hurt. I want to tell you something. You can be relieved of that fear once and for all when you are married to a Christian husband, for a Christian husband understands his role. In relation to the wife, Paul said to the husband, "Husbands, love your wives, even as Christ also loved the church, and gave himself for it" (Eph. 5:25). The wife does not submit herself to her husband in order to be dominated by him, or to lose her identity, or to merely assume the role of a housekeeper. A wife gives herself to her husband for the same reason the husband gives himself to his wife. The reason is that is the way of love, and if you don't understand that you're in trouble at the start. If you've never comprehended the love of God in Jesus Christ, you don't have the foundation for building a happy, lasting, Christian home. When you do comprehend, neither husband nor wife loses identity through submission to the other. This is God's way and God's way is right. It has forever been proven to be true.

Jesus loved the church and gave himself for her. He asked not what the church could do for him; he asked what he could do for the church. He loved and served and protected the church. One day he's coming back to claim the church as his holy bride.

Listen friend, if you love your wife in that way, your wife will never fear to submit herself to you as unto the Lord. A woman does this, becomes submissive in the role of wife and mother, as a manifestation or a revelation of her relationship to Christ. When she does it on that basis, she doesn't hold back anything. The giving is unreserved; it is in totality; and there's nothing kept selfishly.

When a husband loves his wife like Christ loves the church, he loves her with all of his being. Nothing is exempt. The husband is the head of the wife in the same way Christ is head of the church. Friends, when that relationship exists it rules out neglect, abuse, or dictatorial arrogance.

I wish every young person would sit up and listen to this: You are not ready for marriage until you are mature enough to want to give yourself to another for the well-being of the other person. That's what love is all about. You're not ready for marriage until you're ready to deny yourself and give yourself to another. You're in trouble at the outset if you marry an egocentric, self-seeking individual, who's going to be ruthless in his desire to exalt himself and step on anyone in order to gain his own way.

I've got news for the girls who think marriage is a reform school where you can reform that "ole boy." There are a lot of people in our world who would stand and laugh at you for thinking such a ridiculous thought. They found out the hard way that it isn't. If he drinks before you marry him, he'll probably keep on drinking. If you want to know what kind of person your husband or wife to be will be, look at his parents, look at her parents. That's the way to find out. The chances are excellent that they'll grow up to be just like the ones who nurtured them, who gave them life, who taught them and trained them.

If a husband loves his wife like Christ loves the church, it is an elevating love. The Lord Jesus desires every member of the body of Christ to reach his highest potential. Christ doesn't want you to be second-rate. He wants you to be your best for him, for his kingdom, and for society. Your best may not be comparable to someone else's best, but Christ wants you to be your best. Now, friend, if you love your wife in that way, you're going to want her to be the best person, the best wife, the best mother she can possibly be. You'll give yourself to that attainment day by day. If the love of a husband for his wife is real, then that love is going to follow the divine pattern. It will be an elevating love.

Christ's love for his church is a providing love. In that love he made provision for every need the church would ever have. Do you hear me? Every need of the church throughout the age until Christ returns is guaranteed by the presence and power of his Holy Spirit. A husband who loves his wife will be interested in and provide for her every need; physical, material, intellectual, and spiritual. That's the way Christ provides for his church because of his love for us. Through the power of the Holy Spirit every need we have is supplied.

You know, I've never known a husband and a wife who were totally committed to the happiness of each other who had trouble in their home, trouble between themselves, or trouble with their families. A husband who is totally committed to the well-being and the happiness of his wife and a wife who is totally committed to the well-being and the happiness of her husband just don't encounter the kinds of problems that lead to a divorce court. Now there may be other kinds of problems. There may be illnesses, sorrows, and tragedies that come, but when those two stand together as one flesh under God, they can meet any emergency life brings and meet it victoriously in the Spirit of Christ. The husband is the head of the house. In his relationship to his wife, he must understand what that involves.

Now think, if you will, of a father's relationship to his

Wealth.

Surveys indicate that the average individual in America is assaulted by a minimum of 560 advertising messages every day. Would you believe that? Yes, it's easy to believe if you just stop and think a moment. Out of these 560 messages with which he is bombarded daily, he notices only 76 of them. Do you understand what that says? That says a human being blocks out 484 advertising messages and reserves his attention for other things.

If you wives ever think your husband has the capacity to "tune you out," you had better thank God for that capacity or these advertisements would run him crazy! Sometimes he can sit there and be in another world while you're talking to him, and all of sudden you say, "You're not listening to me!" That never happened to anybody else, did it? Well, I expect it did, and this is the defense mechanism all of us build up. With these advertisements being thrown at us, hitting us between the eyes, we block out of the 560 all except 76. That means we choose to ignore the vast bulk of those things paraded before us. That's a human right. I have the inherent right as a human being to ignore trivia, and I still have that push button control on my television. Every time a beer commercial comes on, I push it off. I don't watch or listen to trivia. Now I may not have any control over what they put on the tube, but thank God I've got control over what comes into my den! If I don't want it, I'll cut it off! I don't care how catchy the tune is or how beautiful the scenery, I turn it off, I mute it when it comes on.

We're bombarded every day with advertisements of every kind, but tragically some human beings are giving their attention to trivia and overlooking things that really matter. Some have tuned in completely to material things and are literally selling their souls for what the world has to offer. That includes the pleasures and recreation of this world, which though valid in place, can become a god for you and me. If you think the epitome of life, the *summum bonum* of it all, is to have a three-car garage with two new cars and a boat, then you're the one to whom I'm talking. If you think that money is life's highest goal and you're spending yourself to amass a certain amount in certificates of deposits, or in saving accounts, or a certain portfolio of stocks and bonds, and things of this kind, you're the one to whom I'm talking. You're giving your life for things that don't last! That's the ultimate foolishness—to spend your days and hours on this earth, as limited as they are, for things that don't amount to a hill of beans.

Let me remind you that God's Word teaches that "A good name is rather to be chosen than great riches" (Prov. 22:1). Did you hear it? Do you believe it? "A good name is rather to be chosen than great riches." Let me tell you something. There are some persons whose names are unknown in financial circles, who when they stand before God in judgment are going to have riches and wealth this world could never touch. There are some who may not be able to write a check for a hundred dollars who nevertheless have a good name, and when they pass on they'll be remembered for that to which they gave themselves. A good name is rather to be chosen than great riches.

The best thing you can leave your children is not a bundle of money they can fight and squabble over, nor property that they can go to court and argue over, but a good name and the memory of a life committed to things that really matter.

You see, the head of the house has a direct relationship to wealth and if your wealth is what the coin of this realm can purchase, then your wealth is going to pass on when you die. If your wealth consists of things that live forever, then your good name will live forever.

Think now of the head of the house in regard to his

Witness.

Every home deserves a head who has seriously considered life's alternatives. "Seriously considered" means involved in a serious study of the claims of Jesus Christ and his church. You're not a fit head of a house until you've weighed the alternatives.

When Richard Hogue approached high school students in their assembly programs he did it on this basis: "There is a spiritual dimension in life that most of you have overlooked, and you owe it to yourself to check this out. I'm saying not only high school students but also many heads of houses have failed to check out the spiritual dimension in life. All you know about Christ is what you've heard someone else say. All you know about the Word of God is what someone else said."

Somebody asked me the other day on the telephone,

"Preacher, where do you find that Scripture, 'Every tub sits on its own bottom?' " That's about all some people know about the Scripture! "Oh, I know it's in the Bible," she said. You've listened to a lot of people, but have you checked it out yourself? Have you ever put yourself at the disposal of the living Christ? Have you ever dared to say in total sincerity, "Lord Jesus, if you're really alive I want you to be revealed to me." Friend, I dare you to do that. But if you do, you'd better fasten your seat belt for you're in for the ride of your life! He'll reveal himself to you so quickly and with such great clarity that you'll know it is a miracle come from God!

Plato is reported to have said that the life of the nation is only "the life of the family writ large." College students sleeping off their hangovers on Sunday mornings, sexual immorality of every kind from youngsters junior high age and up, and the lack of integrity in government circles is but an enlarged photograph of the American home today. Those are the sort of things our homes produce.

If the father is the head of the house, the major burden of responsibility for the home and its spiritual direction is placed at his door. I hope you're listening to this. For the most part we've turned this over to the wife. Religion is for the women and the kids. Big deal! That shows how little we know about Jesus Christ and his followers.

Out of the twelve apostles there was not a single woman involved. Out of those to whom he committed the responsibility for the ongoing of the kingdom, the basic responsibility was in the hands of the twelve, who became eleven, and then became twelve once again. The religion of Jesus Christ is for men in positions of leadership, showing the way for others to follow.

It's a sad day in your home and in our nation when the women have to assume the responsibility for spiritual leadership. The father is responsible before God, because he is assigned the privilege and obligation of being the head of the house.

One day a policeman noticed a man standing on a busy street corner in one of our large cities, his face covered with tears. The policeman walked up to him and asked kindly, "Are you in trouble? Is there anything I can do?"

The man's answer shocked the officer. "No sir, I'm not in trouble, but whenever I come to this city I come to this corner and stand awhile. I usually end up crying and thanking God for what happened in this place."

Then the man told this story.

"I was leaning up against this wall about half drunk when a man passed by and looked hard at me. He turned and came back and asked, 'Aren't you Billy Sunday the baseball player?' I told him I was."

"He just stood there a few moments and then he said, 'I'm glad my boy is not with me. To him you're a hero, and I'd hate for him to see you now.' The man walked away. Presently the Salvation Army came and held a street service."

Then Billy Sunday said, "I listened to their songs and to the sermon and I followed them to their hall and that very night I gave my heart to God. I never dreamed I was worth anything to anybody."

Listen to me, father, head of the house, your witness is worth much to many. Your influence is a lengthening shadow that touches innumerable lives. You are to love your wife like Christ loved the church, but before you can love her that way you've got to love him with a deep and lasting love. When you get that vertical relationship properly established, the horizontal relationship will fall in its proper place.

I'm sure many of you remember the admonition of William Cullen Bryant in his poem "Thanatopsis."

> So live, that when thy summons comes to join
> The innumerable caravan which moves
> To that mysterious realm, where each shall take
> His chamber in the silent halls of death,
> Thou go not, like the quarry-slave at night,
> Scourged to his dungeon, but, sustained and soothed
> By an unfaltering trust, approach thy grave
> Like one who wraps the drapery of his couch
> About him, and lies down to pleasant dreams.

What a challenge that is. A challenge to make those footprints wide and deep and straight, pointing in the right direction, pointing others to God in Christ Jesus, whom we know and whom we live to serve.

8. When Free Men Stand

Psalm 33:12

Our American freedoms were not born in Philadelphia, Pennsylvania, on July 4, 1776. Our freedoms date back to England. They have their roots in Western Europe. They can be traced back further to Rome and then across the Mediterranean world to Athens, and from Athens up the Mediterranean seacoast to Jerusalem, and then southward to the Sinai Peninsula and to Mount Sinai itself.

But it was a new kind of national freedom born in Philadelphia on July 4, 1776. That was the date on which the Declaration of Independence was issued, but from the declaration to the independence lay a long, blood-stained journey. The interval was marked by war, wounds, agony, death, prison, and destitution.

The Declaration of Independence is based on one unchanging premise. That principle, written so clearly in our original American document, is that every human being derives his inalienable rights from the owner and operator of this universe, Almighty God, who revealed himself in Jesus Christ. This thread runs through our history in an unmistakable fashion. This foundational premise is valid today because God is who he is and we are who we are. The purpose of a government under God is to guarantee and protect the rights of individuals.

In ancient history Pericles built a civilization upon culture; it failed. Caesar built a civilization upon military might; it failed. Our forefathers founded a civilization upon faith in God, and our nation will survive only so long as it honors the God who is central in our history and our documents. Our forefathers established this nation upon that one unalterable belief.

The Declaration of Independence exalts faith in God and the dignity of man. This very brief document contains only 1,321 words. The average reader can read it in eight minutes. In the text of the Declaration, God is mentioned twice at the beginning and his name is found twice toward the end. Faith in God produced that document. Faith in God launched this nation on her illustrious career.

In the pages of the Old Testament, we find outstanding characteristics of the prophets of God. One of these characteristics is that these prophets continually called people to a recognition of their heritage. Prophetic preaching was a reminder to them of who they were. Prophetic preaching, in the words of Isaiah, was "Look unto the rock whence ye are hewn and to the hole of the pit whence ye are digged" (Isa. 51:1). In that spirit I come, in a manner I trust is prophetic, calling all of us to look anew to the rock from whence we were hewn, to recall those beginnings from which we have grown.

We stand as free men today. Whether our sons, grandsons, and great-grandsons will stand as free men depends in great measure upon you and me. We are free. Whether they shall be free depends upon our attitude toward and our commitment to the preservation of freedom.

Let me call upon free men to stand and look at

Tyranny.

Love for freedom and opposition to tyranny caused men to stand in 1776. They pledged their lives, their fortunes, and their sacred honor to one another for the common cause.

I wonder how many of us in the United States today would pledge our lives, our fortunes, and our sacred honor for the good of others. Not for the advancement of self, but for the good of all, for the sake of the whole, for the perpetuation of our nation.

It was that indominable spirit that prompted Nathan Hale to speak his immortal words, "I only regret I have but one life to lose for my country." Hale was not in a worship service when he said that. It was not in a time of national peace and worldwide tranquillity, but it was on the occasion when he was about to be hung as a spy. Our enemies, at that time, had convicted him, and he was giving his life for your sake and mine.

The thrilling episode of Paul Revere at Concord and the Old North Church is a saga of resistance to tyranny. My heart was thrilled recently as we crossed a bridge on the Charles River and looked to see the steeple on the Old North Church. I am profoundly impressed with what has taken place in our history and the sacrifice that has been made for us.

It's certainly true that at Lexington a shot was fired which was heard around the world. To think that tyranny was decisively and forever defeated at the end of the Revolutionary war is to misunderstand its insidiousness. Like a beard, tyranny returns daily and must be fought continually.

Our Lord faced the temptations of Satan in concentrated form in the wilderness. That did not exhaust the temptations or the efforts of Satan to lure our Lord into sin. Jesus Christ had a daily battle with Satan, just as you and I. That same thing is true regarding tyranny. The fight against tyranny is continuous. No generation will ever be exempt from this struggle because human nature is what it is. Until human nature in general, in totality, is transformed by the power of God and becomes what God designed it to be, the fight against tyranny must continue.

I believe a vast majority of Americans remember the Maine, the Alamo, Argonne Forest, and Pearl Harbor. When those calls for freedom came in other generations, Americans answered, they stayed till it was over, over there. They came home in honor. This includes Flanders' Fields, the rocks of Corregidor, the bleak slopes of Korea, and the steaming, vermin-infested jungles of Vietnam. Americans have stood when the time came for free men to stand. Whether or not that will continue depends upon us.

The subject for this message came from a line of our beloved national anthem. "Oh, thus be it ever when free men shall stand,/Between their loved homes and the war's desolation." That's why America is here today. In every generation free men have dared to stand, to put their lives on the line for values more important in the long-range perspective than those immediate values to which we so often respond. I don't believe that old-fashioned American patriotism is dead. I believe Americans would respond instantaneously to any aggressive act of tyranny against us.

Recently we sat in the galleries of the United States Senate in our nation's Capitol. We were there at 10:00

o'clock when the Senate convenes. Unfortunately, and I believe to our shame, there were only two senators on the floor when the opening prayer was offered. It's my belief that those two were there because they were to speak at the outset. They spoke, though there were no other senators present to hear them. Their burden was the fact that the president was leaving that day on a trip that would take him to Moscow and other strategic spots on this earth. They wanted the Soviets, with the rest of the world, to know that our president would not be speaking from a vantage point of weakness, but from strength. Both senators were on the Democratic side of the aisle, but they stood unapologetically to state that they supported the Republican president of the United States in his mission. They wanted our enemies to know that this nation would not tolerate aggression or tyranny. Thank God that spirit still exists. I pray it will permeate our nation as it did in 1776.

The tyranny we face is not all on the outside. Sometimes it is on the inside, often in the form of those little men whose major purpose in life is to make money. They make it, whether it means selling dope or alcoholic beverages or anything else that enslaves the minds and lives of human beings and debilitates personalities made in the image of God! Sometimes little, self-seeking individuals are the tyrants who play the tune to which we march in cadence. Free men must stand today against all tyranny.

Sometimes that tyranny is seen in the form of unreasoning prejudice. It is seen in the form of aggressive self-assertion, elbowing any and everyone out of the way in order to achieve one's own goals. Tyranny returns daily. It must be fought constantly.

Free men must stand not only against tyranny but also against

Tragedy.

I'm not one of those who believes that love is blind. I believe the opposite, for God is love and God is not blind to my sin. He loved me while I was yet a sinner and Christ died for me! Love is not blind. Love evaluates, knows, and sees faults, foibles, frailties, and failures. So it is in that spirit you and I carry on a lover's quarrel with our country. I love America as you do. Though I love this land, I am not blind to her faults.

In our families we debate about the food budget, we bicker over our discipline of the children, we disagree about the dent in the fender of the new car, but our love for one another is not at stake. In that spirit I want to point out some of the tragedies I feel exist in our society.

Perhaps the first and greatest tragedy is indifference. It is no new thought to be reminded that *U.S.* spells us. No nation will ever rise above its people, and you and I are the nation. No chain will be stronger than its weakest link, and we are links in the chain. Frankly, self-interest has become the god of our lives, both in society and in the work of the kingdom of God.

Why is it that churches all over the Northeast have closed? It is because of a lack of interest. The graffiti on the back of the door to our church balcony says, "This balcony is closed." Someone added underneath, "due to a lack of interest." Self-interest becomes the dominant theme in our lives. This is true in regard to the church and the kingdom of God, and it's true in regard to our nation. We oppose anything that runs counter to our personal likes and dislikes. If it affects us adversely, we immediately rise in indignation to oppose it. We're not concerned for the good of the whole; we're concerned about what affects us. I wonder how long this nation can exist with that sort of spirit. Until some of us become big enough to get interested in the good of the corporate body, the body politic, we may be assured we are on a toboggan slide downward toward destruction.

That's exactly what Isaiah said to the people of his day: "All we like sheep have gone astray; we have turned every one to his own way" (53:6). Brother, that's our generation. We're looking out for number one, and if we don't like something, we oppose it. If it causes a change in our schedule or our routine, we won't have anything to do with it. Self-interest is a tragedy in regard to national interests.

Our nation was founded by men who believed in God, in individual freedom, in high moral values, and personal responsibility. Here is where we fail. We can't fight successfully against evil when three-fourths of the army is AWOL. This church as an institution in the kingdom of God will never succeed when we gather on Sunday night with three-fourths of the people absent, because of their self-interest. You can count on battles like that being lost.

Another part of the tragedy is idleness. We refuse to become involved, and little do we suspect that noninvolvement is the cancer eating away at the heart of America.

One of the wonders of the world is the Great Wall of China, which extends for more than two thousand miles along the border between Mongolia and China.

It was built in the third century B.C. by an emperor who utilized three hundred thousand workers, most of whom were prisoners. The wall was twenty to fifty feet high. It was between fifteen and twenty-five feet thick. It had towers at regular intervals. The interesting thing is that wall was never bridged in combat by any enemy. Nobody ever stormed that wall. They didn't have to. They bribed the gatekeepers and came through without having to force an entrance. This is the natural result of idleness and refusal to become involved; it is failure to stand in the gap when the battle is taking place.

Let me mention another part of the tragedy. Let's call this one inflation, and it is something with which we live every day. The major reason for inflation, in my judgment, is government spending. In a recent survey taken in the Washington, D.C. area, 78 percent of the people wanted Congress to pass a law placing a ceiling on annual government spending and to make it a crime for congressmen to exceed that ceiling. I can guarantee that would have a beneficient effect upon the inflationary spiral if it could ever be done.

The National Taxpayers Union, which is a nationwide organization, is protesting such items in the federal budget as $375,000 for a Pentagon study of the Frisbee. You know what a Frisbee is? Items such as $159,000 to teach mothers how to play with their babies. Or $121,000 in the national budget to find out why some people say "ain't," $20,234 in the national budget for a study of the mating calls of the Central American toad. I think we have passed the ridiculous point in some governmental programs. We've learned to pray with facility, "Our father, who art in Washington," and we are looking to Uncle Sam to provide everything we want

from the cradle to the grave. Let us remember the wisdom of Abraham Lincoln who said, "That government
is best that governs least."

When free men stand, we must stand against tyranny,
against the tragedies of the present, and we must stand
together in

Trust,

and I mean trust in Almighty God. Now, don't confuse
this with trust in our religious culture. Don't confuse
this for trust in the religious remnants that can still be
found in our society, vestiges left over from another
generation, such as putting on our coins "in God we
trust."

Nearly every president in his inaugural address has
made reference to God or to divine providence, but
trust in America and in the laws of our society is not
adequate. We've been taught, as Americans, that law
is greater than the individual, and that philosophy goes
back to the ancient Greeks. Justice is pictured as standing
blindfolded with a scale in her hand. This is symbolic
of man's equality before the law. The ideal of justice
is summed up in the words of Solon, the lawmaker,
who said, "(Law) smooths what is rough, checks greed,
dims arrogance, makes straight the crooked government, tones the deeds of insolence and ends the wrath
of bitter strife." What a glorious, high sounding pro-
nouncement. The fact is, for the Spartan Helot, it was
not so; for the Roman galley slave, it did not prove
true. For the serf on the feudal estate, law did not give
him equality; for the Jews in the days of the Spanish
Inquisition, there was no equality. For the Puritan in
Stuart England, there was nothing but persecution and

death. For the Negro bound in the chains of slavery here in America, there was no equality under law. Our trust must be in God's laws, not man's laws!

When free men stand tall they bend their knees before Almighty God. A nation never stands taller or more erectly than when it bends low before its Maker. That's the reason America has been great, and unless that reason prevails again, America's greatness is in the past and not the future.

During the dark days of World War II, Winston Churchill was invited to return to Harrow, the preparatory school which he attended as a boy. The headmaster reminded all of the students to be sure to bring their pencils and notebooks to record the words of this world famous statesman. When Churchill, that gallant warrior, stood, he said, "Never give in. Never give in. Never! Never! Never!" then turned and was seated.

I believe the words of Churchill have an application today. With unswerving faith in God and abounding confidence in our nation, with trust in one another, we say today, never quit trying! Never give up! Never stop working! Never cease witnessing. Never! Never! Never as long as God gives us breath! With that spirit America, under God, will be one nation indivisible.

9. Our Common Glory

1 Corinthians 3:8–9

From a secular, pagan viewpoint work is looked upon as a necessary evil which holds everyone in its grip except a few extremely rich people. This attitude has pervaded our nation and perhaps a great part of the world in which we live.

It has been estimated that by retirement, each one of us will have invested 125,000 hours in work, occupying ourselves in some labor in order to gain a livelihood. This is a significant segment of life, but it is serious and tragic in light of an astonishing statement which I recently read. A writer stated the majority of adults in this country hate their work. For most Americans work is mindless, exhausting, boring, servile—something to be merely endured.

Maybe someone has already asked, "Well, where is the preacher going with this? What direction is he taking? What does the Christian gospel have to do with what he has said?" Let me remind you on this Labor Day weekend that work is honorable, noble, and exalting, and there is no possibility for so significant a segment of life as 125,000 hours to be exempt from the influence of the Christian gospel. In fact, there is no minute in life for a Christian that is not under the demands of the Christian faith. There is no vacation from

God; there is not time out from the Christian faith or
living for Christ; and there's no area of life from which
we can exclude our Lord.

Because of that, I want to address myself to this all-
important topic, "Our Common Glory." I trust you look
upon the work you perform daily as a glorious work,
a challenge, an opportunity, a place in which you can
make an investment of yourself that will bring eternal
dividends.

Let's look first at our

Calling.

It's high time we explode that age-old myth that work
is a curse. This theory goes back to the Garden of Eden
and holds that labor is a product of man's fall, that Adam
and Eve in their original sinless estate fell and were
under the sentence or curse of God to gain their livelihood by the sweat of their brow. There are many people
who believe they have to work today because of sin. A
closer look at the Bible in its entirety will reveal a totally
different picture.

Going back to the author of it all, God himself is a
working God. The Greek philosophers pictured him as
a do-nothing God, seated out in space with his chin
on one hand, his elbow in his other hand, thinking. God
was a thinker in their concept. Yet every chapter in the
Word of God reveals that he is an active, working God,
and it began in creation. In creation God made you
and me in his own image. That simply reminds us that
even as our Creator is a working being, we too are to
be working beings. Adam's sin caused a change in his
nature, not a change in his work.

We are not just called to work on earth, we're looking

forward to existence in eternity where we will continue
to serve. A lot of people think heaven is going to be
an eternal morning of sleeping late, being able to turn
over, turn off the alarm clock, and go back to sleep.
That's going to be heaven some think, just not to have
anything one must do. To have days and hours and
aeons of eternity in which there are no demands made
on one whatever! Listen, the Bible makes no such claim
and paints no such picture. We're not going to be carried
to the skies on flowery beds of ease for a life of meaningless existence. Relevation 7:15 states, "Therefore are
they [that is, God's redeemed] before the throne of God,
and they serve him day and night" The redeemed serve
God—continuing activity, meaningful labor and existence, contributing something, having the satisfaction
that comes through knowing one has made and is making
a meaningful contribution. Those persons who are dissatisfied with life today are sometimes older people, re-
tired from all active labor. They find life to be intolerable
because they have lost the significance of work. After
a lifetime of routine and schedule and daily investment
of personality in a particular labor, suddenly they are
relieved of all of this and life becomes insipid, flat, and
tasteless for them.

The chief means of achievement in our world is by
finding meaning in one's lifework. If you find no meaning in the work you are doing, it's little wonder if you
have an acid view of life.

It has been said that he who works only with his hands
is a laborer. He who works with his head and hands is
a craftsman, but he who works with his head, hands,
and heart is an artist. My friends, you don't have to
hold a palette in your hand or a brush between your
fingers to be an artist.

Let me share an experience from my first pastorate. I was pastor of a country church in rural south Mississippi. There was a man, a member of the church, who had been elected to the post of county commissioner. He had miles and miles of rural gravel road in his district. He had an employee known all over that county. This man drove a motor grader, but he was a consummate artist in doing his job. When a road was being graded or when additional gravel was being added, or a new road being built, oftentimes there would be groups of people who came out to watch him operate that motor grader. He knew precisely how to do his job, and he had his heart in it. He loved his work. There was a look of pride upon his face when the end of the day would come and he would step down off the motor grader to make his way home. Not only were his hands and head involved but also his heart was in it.

Whatever task you may fill, whatever position you may hold, you have an opportunity to be artistic in it by giving the totality of your being. That's your calling. You don't have to be in a church related vocation to be called of God. You don't have to be a preacher or a minister of education or a minister of music. You can fill any honorable position in life under divine orders! God calls people into many different places.

If you are dissatisfied with your present occupation, if you are unhappy at the place where you work, the chances are you have a job and not a calling. Your calling does involve the assurance that you are in the will of God. If we were to take a poll and every person were honest, how many persons responding would be able to say with joy, "Yes, I am in God's will in the job I now have"?

It's been said that a mere job has three characteristics.

First, we want to get it over with the least possible effort. Second, we want to finish it in the shortest possible time; three, we want as much pay for it as we can possibly get.

Americans by and large seem to have lost pride in their work. There was a time, years ago, when the label "made in the United States of America" conveyed a certain sense of pride and a degree of excellence. During that period in our history, any article labeled "made in Japan" was looked down upon and sneered at. But today any article labeled "made in Japan" is likely an article that carries a certain integrity. It's made to last, a quality article; whereas, many of those things that are made in the United States of America are admittedly inferior. What has happened? Whatever it is goes back ultimately to the laborers, those who make the products, those who lose their pride in producing quality articles. We not only make articles in a shabby fashion but also many of them today are produced with built-in obsolescence. They are not designed to last. They are designed to function only for a brief period of time.

If we had enough time for a testimony meeting, we'd have people all over who would bear testimony to their dissatisfaction and unhappiness with a new car which was a "lemon." Everything went wrong with it.

I remember the irritation I experienced when the twenty-four-month guarantee on my car battery ran out, and two days later the battery had to be replaced! Boy, it was made to last twenty-four months and that's all.

If I were to ask you to give testimony concerning a major appliance you bought that was defective from the beginning, we'd have people everywhere saying, "Yes, I've had that experience. I've been there. I know what

that's all about.'' This indicates a lack of pride in work-
manship, and it's an affliction that has become a plague,
an epidemic over our nation.

A major mazagine sometime ago had an article which
suggested that when buying a new automobile, you
ought to make every effort to determine on what day
of the week it was produced. That article warned con-
sumers not to buy a new car produced in the factory
on Monday, Tuesday, or Friday. The reason being that
the workers are "hung over" after a weekend and are
not really alert to what they are doing on Monday and
Tuesday. And by the end of the week they are looking
forward to the weekend; they get in a big hurry and
do a shabby job. I don't know if that is true, but that's
what the article said.

There is a big difference between a job and a calling.
A calling is something that you can no more keep from
doing than you can keep from breathing. It includes a
kind of eagerness for one's responsibilities that makes
the hours fly by and sounds the trumpets every morning
to get one out of bed.

I talked last week with my good friend Harper Shan-
non, pastor of a church in Birmingham and author of
a book entitled, *Trumpets in the Morning.* He was describ-
ing his feeling of call and sense of commitment to that
responsibility God has given him. He said it was like
hearing trumpets every morning, wanting to get out of
bed, wanting to get to work, not being able to wait until
he got to work to fulfill his responsibilities. Do you have
this kind of feeling? I thank God I hear trumpets every
morning! I have a deep feeling of love for that which
God has called me to do, and the assurance that I am
in the will of God right now.

Robert Louis Stevenson's philosophy was this: "If a man love the labor of his trade apart from any consideration of success or fame, the gods have called him." Winston Churchill once said there were two kinds of people. First, there are those for whom work is work and pleasure is pleasure. Then the other kind, he said, are those for whom work and pleasure are one. Is that your feeling? Do you have that attitude toward the position you occupy in the business world? For those whose work is pleasure, no day is ever long enough. Every day is a holiday. Work is joyous and when ordinary holidays come they are looked upon as enforced interruptions from an absorbing vocation. We hate for a holiday to come because we don't have an opportunity to do our major task. There is a big difference between a job and a calling.

Let me talk with you about some

Conditions

that exist in our nation. Many factors contribute to the sordid mess in which we find ourselves. Welfare has gradually become an acceptable career in America, that is, if you have no conscience and no pride. You can get by well in our welfare state if you don't have any personal ambition, no desire to be something for the benefit of other people. Actually, welfare is a rather secure way of life, but it is also secure to be an inmate in a penitentiary. Everything is provided. No worry about clothes, food, income, taxes—everything is provided for you. For many people that might be acceptable, but for a Christian it has no place in one's life. Politicians will weep over you if you are an object of welfare and big crocodile tears will stream down their cheeks. The state will give a woman who has the ability to bear children a bonus for each illegitimate child she produces.

In any direction in which we look we are faced with the menace of mediocrity. Talk with any employer in any city and he will tell you that his biggest task is to try to find someone who will work, someone who will accept responsibility and who can be counted on to do what he said he'd do. Mediocrity is a way of life for far too many of us.

Larry Brumfield, writing in a recent issue of *Guideposts Magazine,* recalled an experience which was his when a college freshman. He had taken a course in calculus, in which he had no interest. His grandmother happened to be at his home the day the grades arrived in the mail. He was looking at his grades and explained to his grandmother that the C which he made in calculus actually was a pretty good grade. But his grandmother, with the wisdom born of age, reminded him that a C was just as close to the bottom as it was to the top. Most of us would be content with that, right in the middle, right on the average, mediocre!

The menace of mediocrity threatens us continuously. Young people and adults are confronted with it. A youth just completing his education and applying for a job is concerned primarily with one thing: how much does it pay? what are the fringe benefits? how much time off do I get? how long is my paid vacation? If that's all we are living for, we cannot claim to be followers of Christ. If that's the ultimate in your life, then you've missed Christ somewhere back down the road.

Take a schoolteacher, for instance. One schoolteacher makes the same salary as every other teacher in the school who has the same education and experience. Ability means nothing. The tendency is to look around and say, "This one, who is making just as much as I am, is not working nearly as hard as I am. Though I have skills and abilities others don't have, I'll not use them because they have not been recognized by an added remuneration." The temptation for all of us is not to rise above the quality of those around us, regardless of the ability that God may have given us. We are inclined to do as much as others who make the same amount of salary.

We live in an era of the great goof-off, the day of the half-done job. An advertising executive pointed out that we live in a land populated by laundrymen who refuse to iron shirts, waiters who will not serve tables, carpenters who have forsaken their tools. There are executives whose minds never get off the golf course, laborers who demand a minimum salary wage regardless of their ability or their achievement, teachers who expect a single fixed income irrespective of ability and effectiveness. Workmen in every field are interested in wages, not in work! What a commentary!

Does the Christian faith say anything to you and me in this situation? You'd better believe it! The way you respond to the responsibilities you have, for which you are remunerated, is the way a lot of pagans evaluate Jesus Christ. They say, "If he's a Christian, I don't want any part of it. If that's how a Christian acts, taking advantage of the employer, doing a shabby job, coming to work late and leaving early, and looking for every rat hole he can run down—you can keep your Christianity." My friend, we do not honor Jesus Christ when we accept a job and don't fulfill it to the best of our ability.

How are we going to handle a problem like this, living in a society that expects and demands less and less of us? We are talking now about a thirty-hour week. Maybe the day will come when they will talk about a twenty-hour week. We don't want to work! We haven't found our common glory. We haven't been turned on by the fact that we are in God's will, and we are doing something that has significance not only for ourselves and our families but also for other people. How are we going to handle this thing?

The answer to it is

Commitment.

The way out of this situation is to make demands upon ourselves. Not the demands society makes, but the demands we make because we know Jesus Christ. The only way open to you and me to find lasting joy in doing a job well is to do it to the utmost of our capabilities. My best may not be *the* best. There may be myriads who can perform a particular job far better than I, but that's not the point. The point is, am I doing my utmost in my job? If I am, I can go home after work with joy, peace of mind, and contentment, knowing that I've made the best investment I am capable of making. There are things undone, things that have had to be left out, but if I have functioned to the best of my capability, I can go home with peace toward God and peace toward my fellowman.

One of the saddest comments I have read in many a day was a statement by Jeb Magruder, one of these young men associated with the former national administration, recorded in an issue of *U.S. News and World Report.* He was asked why he did what he did. His answer ought to break the heart of every person who reads it. He said, "My ambition obscured my judgment. Somewhere between my ambition and my ideals I lost my compass." The heartbreak is that has happened to most of us. Somewhere between our ideals, our convictions, and our ambition we've lost the compass. The compass for the Christian is Jesus Christ. When we take our eyes off of him, we may be assured that chaos is the result.

The truth is, all of us need a continuous challenge, and the only challenge we can have that is continuous is to challenge ourselves and to be satisfied personally with nothing short of our best! We have to sanctify our aspirations and make a radical change in the administration of our lives. The chief administrator in your life and mine must be the Holy Spirit of God: when he is in charge, everything we do and say is different.

Recently a critic was berating a preacher whom he said was preaching for money. I asked this person quickly, "What are you working for?" He said, "I'm working for money, but that's different." Is it? It is *not* different for a Christian! A Christian layman has no more right to be working for money alone than does a preacher! That is true whether you like it or not. You haven't got any more right to work for money alone than I have! My calling is spiritual, but there's no difference between my calling and yours! You are called to follow Jesus Christ, not for what you can get out of it, but for what you can give!

I was talking with a man one day who told me about his new assignment and transfer from our city to another city. I asked, "Well, why don't you just stay here?" "Oh, I can't do that," he said. I asked why. He replied, "I've got too much laid up in my retirement, and I'd lose it." Why did he move? For money, m-o-n-e-y. It is equally wrong for a layman or preacher to move just for money. If that's all you are working for, friend, you are missing it. Your commitment is not the highest and best. Yours is not truly a Christian commitment if all you are working for is money. When the Holy Spirit takes over, he causes a change in administration.

There's an ancient story from the time of Caedman, the Venerable Bede, and those boys, centuries and centuries ago, that told of a lonely plowman. He was out in the field all alone plowing. He looked up on the horizon and saw a vast throng of people rushing toward him and a tremendous cloud of dust ascending into the air. As they drew closer he heard their voices. They cried, "Quick, quick. Leave what you are doing. Follow us. The world is coming to an end." He paused for a moment, thought about what they had said, then shrugged his shoulders and replied, "Whether the world is coming to an end or not I do not know, but in the meantime I have plowing to do."

I think all of us agree that Jesus is coming to earth again and the time of his coming may be soon, but until that time comes we've got plowing to do. We've got a job, we've got a calling, a responsibility. God calls every child of his to function at his best, however long he is here on this earth, until that day when God calls him home or until Christ our Lord returns in the air in power.

10. Never, Never Land

Acts 24:25

The annual budget campaign gives us the opportunity to focus upon the sin of procrastination. We don't talk a great deal about this sin, but it's a sin nevertheless. Felix stands in the pages of God's Word as a classic example of this besetting sin. There is not a person on earth who has not succumbed to that sin time and time again.

Most of us pray as it was said Augustine prayed before his conversion, "Lord, make me pure, but not now." This is roughly comparable to a statement I heard attributed to a Methodist bishop. He said the great regret of his life was that he did not visit New Orleans before he became a Christian! Most of us have something of the same spirit. The besetting sin of far too many of us is the sin of living in never, never land. This is when we say, "Yes, I know I ought to but . . . . I know this decision must be made, but not right now."

Someone characterized this sin in these ways: During youth we are too happy to think, believing there is plenty of time. In manhood we are too busy to think, because we're worried over work and health. In the declining years we're too aged to think, for our habits have become rigid and fixed. As death approaches we're too ill to think, for we are weak and suffering. In death it's too late to think, for the die is cast. In eternity, however, we have forever to think, for we must stand God's judgment day.

Like far too many of us today, Felix was living in an unreal world. He was deeply convicted by the words Paul spoke. The text even declared that Felix trembled under the convicting work of God's Holy Spirit. But when it came to the moment of deciding for Christ, Felix said, "Go thy way for this time; when I have a convenient season, I will call for thee" (Matt. 24:25). How like us he was. We come right to the point of decision and then take the coward's way out. We delay, somehow believing that it will be easier or different at some future time. Felix, like many of us, was grasping for that elusive pot of gold at the end of an ethereal rainbow. That convenient day is nothing but a fantasy designed for dreamers and mystics. That convenient season, someday out there in the future, was never intended for achievers who live in a world of reality. It's my prayer that we might come to a sense of reality and make those decisions that must surely be made without any delay.

Let me remind you of some areas in life in which it's tragically easy to procrastinate. The first of these, by far the most important, is

Salvation.

Jesus, when he was here on earth, saw humanity as sheep without a shepherd. How powerfully descriptive! Have you ever stopped to consider how like sheep man really is? Two characteristics of sheep are their defenselessness and their lack of a sense of direction.

History abounds with stories of horses, dogs, cats, and other animals who have been taken a long way from home but who, without any outside help, have been able to find their way home. All of us know of that innate sense of direction possessed by a homing pigeon. Many times these birds are taken hundreds of miles from home and with that unerring, built-in radar they find their way back.

That may be true with some animals and birds, but it's not true with sheep. A sheep has no built-in sense of direction. It can't get back home when lost. That's why in the parable Jesus told, the concerned shepherd went out to find that lost sheep; it was not capable of finding its way back to the fold (see Luke 15:4–6).

When it comes to defenses, most animals have some defense. A dog can bite; a cat can scratch; a horse can kick; and a rabbit can run. Every animal, almost without exception, has some means of defense but a sheep. Isn't that precisely what Jesus was referring to when he saw you and me as sheep not having a shepherd?

Remember the prodigal son. He chose the pleasures of sin for a season. In the Old Testament Moses rejected the pleasures of sin and worldliness that could have been his living in the home of Pharaoh, and he rather chose to suffer affliction with his own people, the people of Israel. The prodigal son chose the pleasures of sin for a season.

Make no mistake about it, there is pleasure in sin. I didn't say joy; I said pleasure. Don't tell young people there's no pleasure in sin. They are too smart for that and so are you. But remind them that there is another side of the coin. Where there may be fleshly pleasures enjoyed in tasting sin, there is also the judgment day of God that is inevitable in which every man must answer for the deeds done in the flesh.

Some time ago on a quail hunt I ran across a quail trap. A quail trap is not a particularly ingenious device, just a very simple means by which a person can trap quail. The quail are trapped alive, and then they are killed and eaten. Leading up to the trap there is scattered grain; inside the trap the grain is heaped up. The quail comes along, just like a man in sin, and finds pleasure in eating the grain. He doesn't have to work for that food. He doesn't have to scratch for seed or other edible particles. Here it is provided for him. Without any thought for the future or for his own personal safety, the quail just keeps eating, getting closer and closer to the trap. Once the quail is inside the trap, after other quail have gathered, the trigger is tripped or the stick is knocked down; the trap falls around those on the inside.

I can think of nothing more descriptive of sin than that. We wander along heedlessly, find something good, and begin to enjoy the pleasure of it without ever looking up and without ever seeing the destination. We never seem to comprehend the fact that there's a trap in which we will become ensnared and which will require our freedom. In the midst of the pleasures of sin, someone has to rise to say there is a judgment day; there is coming inevitably an accounting for every moment spent here in this life. Remember while you sample the pleasures of sin, they are without joy.

You can think not only of the prodigal son's pleasure in sin but also of the poverty connected with sin. Luke 15 says that the prodigal son began to be in want. All the things the prodigal son thought would bring satisfaction, pleasure, and peace of heart left him empty with a meaningless, joyless existence. He thought when he could take his inheritance and spend it the way he wanted there would be an inner satisfaction derived from it. But he found, to his dismay, that sin is not like that.

The possession of sin is also found in the story of the prodigal son. When he wandered away totally defenseless, subject to all the ravages and onslaughts of sin, he suddenly was possessed by sin. Instead of going to the dogs, he went to the hogs, but the end result was the same. This was the lowest point to which a Jewish lad could ever sink. He was forced to attach himself to a citizen of that far, Gentile country. He went to work for a Gentile, which was unspeakable. Not only that but also he was called up to perform a defiling act. He fed a defiling animal, a hog.

Someone has suggested that it is fortunate that the prodigal son didn't live in our generation. If he had, in all probability, a government agency would have appropriated some foreign aid, gone to the far country, built government housing, given this young man a monthly welfare check, and taken care of all his physical needs. As fine as that would have been, to have seen him through his time of physical privation, it would have left no room for repentance and no reason for him to come back home.

This is the modern tragedy. There are a lot of people living in the far country of sin with all physical needs supplied. You have an adequate amount of money, live in a nice home, drive a new car, and have a handsome bank account along with a portfolio of stocks and bonds; but my friend, at some point in this age of affluence, you'd better find your way home. All your physical needs may be supplied in the far country, but there's no government agency nor is there any figure on any greenback that can supply your spiritual need. The only way that need can be supplied is through repentance toward sin and faith in the Lord Jesus Christ. In order to come home one has to turn his back on his sinful condition and start that long, humbling journey.

There are people today who are lost because they prefer to be dignified rather than justified. You may take your dignity with you into the pits of hell unless you come to your senses in time to be justified before death overtakes you.

There are people who are too self-righteous to be saved. They've concluded that the gospel is for the harlot, the crook, the doper, and people in that category. My friend, I remind you that the gospel is for every man, for all have sinned and come short of the glory of God. This is decision day. It's designed for people who are living in that never, never land of fantasy; it is meant to bring you back to a sense of reality and remind you that the only fruit a sinner can produce is repentance. If you've never been saved, there is but one thing in your life God wants and is looking for—the kind of repentance the prodigal son had when he turned his back on the far country and started his long journey home.

This is the day of decision. It is a day of decision in regard to salvation; it is a day of decision in regard to

Stewardship.

The basic factor in Christian stewardship is the new birth. There is no need to talk to people about being good stewards until you talk to them about their relationship to Jesus Christ. Sometimes we get the cart before the horse. We try to get some to be tithers before they are saved. My friends, it won't work that way. It has to work in reverse order; first, you must be born again. When God fixes up a man on the inside, God changes the man's attitude and disposition. If your attitude and disposition are unchanged, there's a real question as to whether God has worked his transforming power in your life. Your words don't prove anything. You see, Jesus said that in the day of judgment there are going to be a lot of people who know the right words. They are going to cry, "Lord, Lord," and they are going to claim to have done many mighty, wonderful things in his name, but to them he'll say, "Depart from me, I never knew you" (see Matt. 25:41). All they have is the right vocabulary. Brother, you can say the right words, you can have the right vocabulary, and still not have anything on the inside. When you have the right thing on the inside, the world's going to know who you are by the way you act, by the way you walk, by the way you talk, and by the way you transact your business. If you transact your business entirely separate from your Christian profession, you've missed something. You've missed something you have no right to miss if you are a Christian.

When God saved you, he didn't save you piecemeal. He didn't save your right hand, then your left foot, then your right eye, then your left ear, then your right foot, and then other parts of your body. When you received Jesus Christ, he came into your life totally and controls life from then on.

You can say the right thing with your lips, you can come down the aisle and know the right formula. You can state glibly, "I received Jesus as my Savior, and I want to be baptized." That's the right thing to say and the right thing to do, but you can say the words without having accepted Christ. There are a lot of people who are going to say, "Lord, Lord," to whom Jesus will say, "I never knew you." Now he will not say, "I knew you once and then forgot you." He will not say, "You once were saved and now you are lost." Jesus didn't say you could be saved today and lost tomorrow. He will say to those mouthing pious platitudes but who are empty inside, "I *never* knew . . . . I didn't know you ever."

Listen, when you claim to be saved the world puts you under a microscope. Don't kick and fuss and fret about it, that's normal, that's natural, and thank God, even lost people know how a Christian ought to act. I'm glad they do and I'm glad they expect it of us. If you've been born from above, you don't have to put on an act. If you've been born from above, you've been saved, and all you have to do is to go about your daily activities in the power of the Holy Spirit living for Jesus. That's not an act, that's a way of life. It isn't something you put on and take off like a garment. It's something you are! And if you aren't that something, you'd better ask yourself if you've ever really been saved.

There's no born-again believer who is too poor to tithe. None. I tithed my first chicken-pickin' dollar! Those who think they are too poor to tithe tend toward laziness, freeloading, and hitchhiking.

But on the other end of the spectrum there is equal danger. In our affluence we tend to deify our possessions; we come to think that we are God; and we dole this money out the way we see fit. We also conclude that the reason we're rich is because we're good, and if other people just worked as hard as we did, they might make it too. We've made it. Now, brother, both of those

extremes are bad and neither one of them can be sub-
stantiated or approved in the teachings of the Word
of God.

Let's just say for a moment, though it is contrary to
fact, that Jesus never mentioned tithing. What does the
New Testament teach apart from tithing? Most all of
us would agree that Jesus said, "Render therefore unto
Caesar the things that are Caesar's; and unto God the
things that are God's" (Matt. 22:21). Now you who have
been born from above, if you're a true believer in Jesus
Christ, tell me, what do you have that really belongs
to God? If you say anything other than everything you
have, there's a question about whether you've been born
from above. "The earth is the Lord's, and the fullness
thereof; the world, and they that dwell therein" (Ps.
24:1). The first thing you learn when you become a
Christian is that you are not your own, you've been
brought with a price; therefore, you must glorify God
in your body.

If you still think that what you have is yours, you'd
better find out what your real relationship to Jesus Christ
is, because if you are withholding something, Christ is
not Lord. Today is an ideal time to face up to and determine the answer to these matters in the Spirit of Christ.
Then if you can tell me that the Spirit of God is leading
you not to tithe, not to be a storehouse tither, you have
refuted the teachings of the Word of God. God does
not deny himself. God's Spirit doesn't lead God's people
in opposite directions. He leads us together to do the
same thing for the honor and glory of our Savior.

Let me suggest one other area of life. Many of us
are living in never, never land on this day of decision
in regard to

Service.

What is your highest motivation for service in the kingdom? Why did you accept a Sunday School class? Were you afraid of pressure from someone or were you afraid that it wouldn't look good if you didn't accept that responsibility? Are you halfhearted and hangdog about it? I want to remind you that the motive for service in the kingdom is the lordship of Jesus Christ.

We have a crying need today for a functional understanding of what the lordship of Christ means. It doesn't mean that we are to sit back with folded hands and wait for him to pick us up by the scruff of the neck and seat of the pants and thrust us into some responsibility. That's not the lordship of Christ at all. You see, the lordship of Jesus Christ and the filling of the Holy Spirit are synonymous. When you really make Christ Lord, you become filled with the Holy Spirit. He's not going to fill you up if you are reserving part of yourself for personal reasons. It's only when you empty yourself of self and give him all that you have and are that he can come and fill you with his Holy Spirit. When Christ is Lord we don't have to beg people to visit, to attend, to witness, to tithe, to fill a vacant responsibility in kingdom service.

I have come to a point in my life and ministry when I don't intend any more to beg and plead and cajole members into service as deacons, Sunday School workers, or other responsibilities. That's getting the cart before the horse. You don't try to get people to *do* something before they *become* something. The emphasis that we make has to be on the new birth and the filling of the Holy Spirit. When we get all who are in positions

of leadership born from above and filled with the Holy
Spirit, we'll have all the people we can utilize for personal visitation, for soul-winning witnessing, for every
other program in the kingdom of God based on the
teachings of the Word of God. No, we don't have to
"crack the whip" and make people feel bad because
they don't visit. The thing we need to do is proclaim
the gospel in such a way that those who aren't saved
will come to know it, and those that have never made
Christ Lord will understand it. When Christ becomes
Lord, the filling of the Holy Spirit comes, and that is
the motive which compels a man to do the will of God!

Unfortunately we have associated the will of God only
with church-related vocations. This is the concept of
the will of God that many laymen have. Listen, the will
of God has far more to do with *character* than it has to
do with *career*. Now I hope you'll understand that, because the will of God has to do with you. Living out
the will of God every day is based on some knowledge
of the future. There is a judgment to face, a hell to
be shunned, and a heaven to be gained.

I know there are some preachers who have taken hell
out of the pulpit, but you better believe God has never
taken it out of the Bible! As long as it's in the Book,
it's still binding and I don't intend to apologize for it.
There are some people who so despise to hear any mention of hell that they will leave one church and join
another. If they've joined one which does not mention
hell, they've joined a church preaching a partial gospel.
It's in the Book, and Jesus had more to say about it
than any other person. Of the numerous appearances
of the word *Gehenna* in the New Testament, most of
the time it's found on the lips of Jesus. Somebody had

better preach about hell and judgment to come.

Death and hell and judgment are as close today as the drunk driver who may run across the center line and hit you head-on. Death and hell and judgment are as close as a stray bullet or a demented holdup man who might take hostages and then eliminate them in his escape attempt. Death, hell, and judgment are just as close as a criminal who may come and break into your home and kill you and every member of your family.

Death is just as close as a cluster of malignant cells or one last heartbeat or some particle of foreign matter found in your bloodstream. Somebody needs to talk about death in regard to service and salvation.

The artist Raphael died with his last picture half-painted. That picture was carried in his funeral procession to remind all the viewers of the uncertainty of life. Franz Shubert died before a symphony was completed. Charles Dickens laid down his pen in the middle of a novel and died.

I want to tell you something. It's not God's will for you to die without a saving faith in Jesus Christ, and I've got Scripture to back that up. The Book tells me that God is "Not willing that any should perish, but that all should come to repentance" (2 Pet. 3:9). If you want to know what God's will is, I'll tell you. It's God's will for you to be saved, to be sanctified, and ultimately to be glorified. If you want to get into the center of God's will today, you can come into that circle through repentance of sin and faith in the Lord Jesus Christ. I can give you scriptural authority for saying today is the day you ought to make that decision. The Bible teaches, "Behold, *now* is the accepted time; behold, *now* is the day of salvation" (2 Cor. 6:2, author's italics).

The longest journey begins with one step. Your Christian pilgrimage, which will stretch out all the rest of your days on earth and then through eternity, begins with a step of faith. You take that first step and when you do, from that moment on as a defenseless sheep without a sense of direction, you will have a Shepherd who knows the way home. That's God's offer.

11. When God's Clock Struck

Galatians 4:4–5

Have you ever paused and wondered why Jesus Christ came in the generation in which he came? Why was it at that particular time God chose to reveal himself in human form? If you've ever pondered this, and if you've ever paused long enough to make a closer study of the historical events surrounding the company of Christ, you've likely been led to the conclusion that the sublimest record ever entered in human annals was the way God converged human events and brought them to a glorious climax in the immortal manger of Bethlehem.

It was not by chance that Jesus came when he did. According to the apostle Paul in our Scripture text, "When the fullness of time was come" (Gal. 4:4). In other words, this was the great climactic event for which God had been preparing human beings from the time of Adam and Eve in the Garden of Eden. This wasn't happenstance; this wasn't something that occurred by accident. Rather, it was God's purpose being fulfilled in God's own time.

At the manger in Bethlehem, we find a Jewish virgin, who under the requirements of Roman law had come in Bethlehem, the city of David, giving birth to a babe. That babe, whose divine life later would be recorded in Greek, was both God and man. Can you imagine the diversity of these elements that were all brought together and focused at the manger in Bethlehem?

That particular age in history had received from the Jewish nation a wealth of religious heritage. The Jews had a religious consciousness that was part and parcel of their lives. They also had faith in the one true and living God. Of all the nations that had arisen through all history, this was the only nation that had consistently been monotheistic. They believed in the one true God whom they designated "the God of Abraham, the God of Isaac, and the God of Jacob." Monotheism was a tremendous contribution to the coming of Christ, who revealed the one true God.

From the Romans that age received an organized world. It was so highly organized that the Romans built a system of roads extending into most all of the known world. Because of that system of roads, because of the Roman legions and their proficiency in military matters, the Romans were able to bring other nations under their dominance. A further indication of the organization of the Romans was that a taxation was made once every fourteen years. One such taxation brought Mary and Joseph to Bethlehem.

From the Greeks in that generation came a highly trained intellect and the most expressive language the world has ever known. It was in the Greek language that God's revelation to man would be recorded in the New Testament.

There was nothing accidental about the coming of Christ, for he came at an appointed hour. He came in God's own time when God's clock struck. God had made ready in his own way. The prophets of the Old Testament had preached of a Redeemer, one who would come and deliver God's people from bondage. Then a star in the heavens led Wise Men to that Redeemer. Angels surrounded the stall where Jesus lay and sang praises concerning him. The shepherds went out from that place and told of him. The apostles later preached Christ, and today every God-called minister upholds and exalts the name of Jesus. He came when God's clock struck.

I would invite your consideration first of history's

Record.

There are other matters related to the birth of Christ which had a direct bearing upon it. Several divergent factors are revealed in this record.

First we must remember Rome and her approach to religion. Keep in mind that officially Rome was polytheistic. Being polytheistic as far as the Christian gospel is concerned is tantamount to being atheistic, having no god. Many gods equal no god. If it takes many gods to suffice in the heart of an individual, he has revealed that the gods he worships are not the one true God, who alone can bring satisfaction and peace.

Rome was tolerant, however, toward religion. Believing in many gods the empire could see nothing wrong with a certain nation worshiping its own god. Consequently, in her approach to the other nations she had brought under her dominance, Rome permitted certain religions to be authorized and made legal. Two terms were used in that day. One was *religio licita,* legal religion, which simply meant that Rome had placed her imprimatur upon that brand of religion and it was legal. They were at liberty to do anything their religion demanded so far as it did not run counter to the decrees of Rome. You can see in the pages of the New Testament, and especially in a study of the book of Acts, how the Christian religion ran counter to Roman decrees. The proclamation of the gospel on the part of the apostles concerning a king and a kingdom other than Rome constituted heresy. It was considered subversion, a direct threat against Rome.

Then there was the other form of religion under the Roman way. It was *religio illicita,* illegal religion. There was no approval given it, and there was an open season on proponents of such a religion. They could be persecuted; they could be hounded; they could be beaten. Anything the authorities wanted to do to such people was all right, because they had no official sanction from Rome.

Judaism, as you can imagine, was *religio licita,* for it was approved. Jews could continue to practice what they believed in the way they wished as long as they did not run counter to Rome. Christianity, on the other hand, was *religio illicita,* and it was always open season on these Christians. These are factors that bear upon God's clock, and its striking at the time that it did.

There's another factor. He was a man. His name was Herod, and he was a king. I believe one of the most interesting psychological studies one could make would be an attempt to discover what kind of person Herod the king actually was. In so far as history reveals this man and his character, he was a greedy, treacherous, foul man with strong paranoid tendencies. I don't suppose that there have been many human beings as despicable as was Herod. He seemed to have a grotesquely distorted view of life. He had an awesome sense of insecurity. His fears were many, whether real or imagined, and this sense of insecurity plus his distortion of life led him to kill all of his enemies and even some members of his own family. When his kinfolk dared to cross him, Herod had no scruples at all about ordering them to their death.

It was this same sort of murderous impulse that led Herod to issue a decree that all the infants in Bethlehem be killed, in order that he might feel secure as king of the Jews. That was the reason Herod tried to get the Wise Men to come back by his court to inform him where they had found this new king; he didn't want any rivals. He couldn't tolerate anyone who might jeopardize his position, and he would resort to killing all babies rather than to run the risk of letting one baby, who might be the King of the Jews, continue to live. You'll recall the New Testament description of the miraculous deliverance of Jesus from this inquisition instituted by Herod.

There's another factor that enters into the record. Let's call this the desire of true Israel. When the decree went out from Caesar Augustus that all the world should be taxed, and each man went into his own native city, there was a gathering, a homecoming, the likes of which we seldom, if ever, have seen. Townsmen who had moved away into other communities were back for the first time perhaps in fourteen years. There was a reunion with those with whom one had grown up, friends and acquaintances over long years, and the topics for conversation were rich and varied. As the people gathered at this time of taxation in small groups in these various cities, they talked about the prospects of trade for the coming year. I feel certain that in those groups gathering all up and down the land in various communities there were those who talked about the true hope of Israel, the coming of the Messiah. That great blessed hope burned so brightly in the hearts of the devout, those who loved God, who believed God's revelation through his prophets of old. So I'm sure there were many who looked for and prayed for the coming of the Messiah. This one God said would be Emmanuel, God with us! For that one they longed, they hoped, and they prayed.

Still another factor that is an integral part of the record centers around Mary, the mother of Jesus. I think we do well to give Mary praise. I think it's unfortunate, however, that the praise of Mary has gone to the point it has in the minds of some. Mary was a human being. Mary was not immaculately conceived. If Mary had been immaculately conceived then there would have been no need for Jesus to come, for she would have won the victory long before our Lord ever appeared on the scene. According to the new Testament, Mary was not immaculately conceived; rather, she was just a humble Jewish maiden like many others. She was virtuous, a virgin. She was pure in her morality and devout in her love of God and her desire to serve him. This young Jewish maiden had received the highest honor of motherhood, that is, God had chosen her to bear his own Son who would be both human and divine, whose name was Emmanuel.

Certainly there must have been conflicting emotions that filled the heart of Mary. She knew beyond any shadow of a doubt what God's angel had said to her. There was no uncertainty about that, no apprehension, no lurking suspicion that it might not be true. She knew God's angel had spoken. But just as surely as she knew this, she also knew what people were saying about her when they gathered in little groups and spoke in whispers behind her back when they saw her in the village.

I don't suppose that there has ever been a human being who has not desired acceptance. I don't know anyone who would not like to be liked. Most all of us would. I'm quite sure there must have been deep consternation in the heart of Mary when suddenly she was confronted with the knowledge of what people were saying. Here she was engaged but not married, and she was expecting a child.

In her heart she knew what God had said, but would people believe it? There may have been some few who did. Thank God Joseph did. Thank God that the way was prepared so that Joseph would believe. But there must have been many, many who didn't believe. What great faith Mary had. Faith greater than you or I would ever possess; for that reason, we need to pay tribute to Mary today, and thank God, that of all the human beings who lived, there was one who would remain constant in her faith. We need to thank God for Mary, who would not waver though people might have gossiped, though people might have criticized, and though it might have been easier to compromise. Thank God for that kind of faith! Thank God for Mary and what she was able to do for the world under the power of Almighty God. When God's clock struck, when the hour came, Mary brought forth her firstborn child, a Son spelled with a capital *S*. She wrapped him in swaddling clothes and laid him in a manger.

All of these factors enter into the record but they come into full culmination in the person of the

Redeemer.

Joy to the world, the Lord has come! Unfortunately

our generation, just like preceding generations, will fail to recognize Jesus. We just won't have time to find out who Jesus is, will we? Oh, we're concerned about inflation, and we're concerned for the political scene. But can we become so concerned with mundane things that we forget what this season is all about? Yes, many prefer to remain at home watching their television sets rather than paying the adoration and devotion of their hearts to the risen Redeemer. We can get so involved in the things of this earth that we don't realize what this season is all about.

Some have come in a critical vein and asked, "Well, is December the twenty-fifth actually the day when Jesus was born?" I don't know, but that's not the point. I'm not so concerned about the externals as I am about the internals. The thought that confronts me is that Christmas is a commemoration of the greatest event that ever transpired in all of history. What difference does it make which day we observe it? We must understand what Christmas was, what it means, and pay our own tribute to it. I would say that if Christians over the world decided that we wanted to commemorate the birthday of Jesus Christ on July the fourth, the commemoration would be the important thing. The event is the important thing, not when, but what.

The same thing is true with the book of Genesis. So many say, "It's not scientific, I don't believe that God made the world in seven days." Well, we don't know what a *day* is. Nowhere in the Old Testament are we told that a day was composed of twenty-four hours, or that an hour was composed of sixty minutes, or that a minute was composed of sixty seconds. The important thing is not how. The important thing is what.

The same thing is true at this Christmas season. We are commemorating the most stupendous event that ever transpired. That's important. Let's not overlook it.

Passing by the manger in Bethlehem in the eyes of our minds, it scarcely seems possible that this is the representation of the greatest power in the world. How can we associate power with a manger? How can we associate power with an impotent babe? Men have never learned to recognize real power.

We talk in terms of hydrogen and cobalt bombs. We talk of the thrust of a Saturn booster that can put a space capsule into orbit around the earth. We think that's the ultimate in power. We talk in terms of earthquakes, tornados, and hurricanes. We speak of the power possessed by the wealthy of our society, and we think we know all there is to know about power. But is anything really powerful if it's incapable of making people happier and worthier?

Weekly we seek to buy our allies from the nations of the world by giving them large appropriations of money. We have come to believe that power is money; our nation, billions and billions of dollars in debt, spends more money, along with the other nations of the world, on armament than has been spent on foreign missions since the day of Pentecost.

Can you describe a billion? Here's the way one person described it. If you had begun on the day that Christ was born in Bethlehem and had spent one thousand dollars per day from then until right now, from that billion you still would have two hundred twenty three million dollars left. Can you reckon a billion?

In the manger in Bethlehem God revealed a power

far greater than anything we can imagine. It was a power so great that a wedge was driven into history, dividing all of time into B.C., before Christ, and A.D., *anno domini.*

The birth of Christ changed the destiny of nations. The birth of Christ, in which there was real power, transformed lives and healed humanity's hurt. But that power was ultimately revealed, not in that manger but in a cross and in an open tomb. And there's still a cross in the heart of God for the sin of mankind. That cross and the One who hung upon it are all powerful, far beyond any power man has uncovered or developed. In that cross, and the One who hung thereon, there's power that can lift the burden of sin from any individual and from all of humanity. That's real power, the power of our Redeemer.

Then a final thing, let's remember our Redeemer's

Return.

When we think of Bethlehem and the fact that God's clock struck there, we also must remember that God's clock is going to strike again. Bethlehem's barn wasn't the last time God's clock would strike. Jesus Christ is to return to this earth and bring to a close all human affairs. Now at Christmas time, when we commemorate the birth of Christ, we must recall our responsibility as Christians and what Christ left for us to do before he comes again.

There are in our day approximately three and one-half billion people in the world. Out in the Orient we have one missionary for every one million people. Can you imagine? In Japan, with a population of approximately one hundred million people, only one person in three hundred is a professing Christian. In Thailand, with twenty-two million people, only one person out of every thirteen hundred is a professing Christian. In our city of over one hundred thousand people, less than 40 percent will be found worshiping on the Lord's Day.

Our Sunday School enrollment is only approximately 50 percent of our total church membership. Our Church Training enrollment is only approximately 50 percent of our average Sunday School attendance. Our prayer meeting attendance is only approximately 50 percent of our Church Training attendance. Oh, my friends, there's much to be done. We haven't yet covered this old earth with the gospel like the waters cover the seas.

In order to prepare for the return of Christ, there must be a radical transformation. Mankind is turned upside down. Our problem is basically this: We have put our hearts where our feet ought to be. Man has set his affection on things of this earth. Our hearts are in the things of this world when in reality we ought to be standing upon this world. Stranger still, man's feet are where his heart ought to be. Man, in his inverted position, is kicking against the God of heaven when he ought to be setting his affection on him.

My friends, God's clock will strike once again. According to the Bible the clock is going to strike when we least expect it. My plea to you today is to decide to serve Christ and follow him right now. Set your affection on things above and put your feet on things of this earth. Will you do it?

12. Mystery of the Ages
Luke 2:1–20

A well-known cliche reminds us, "Familiarity breeds contempt." Even if that cannot be pressed, I think that most of us would be forced to conclude that at the minimum, familiarity breeds indifference.

I well remember living for six years on the Gulf of Mexico, with our home facing Highway 90, the beach, and that beautiful expanse of water. I can also look back and remember day after day, as I drove out the driveway going to work or to other responsibilities, most often I was completely oblivious to the beauty that was there. I was so familiar with it I became indifferent to it.

Sometimes those who live in the mountains tell us that they experience the same thing. As they view the towering peaks around them and in the distance, they often become indifferent to the fantastic beauty. Familiarity breeds contempt or, at the minimum, indifference.

By our very familiarity with the New Testament story of the first Christmas, we've lost much of the aura of mystery that surround it. Yet as we read it again and again, there are mysteries almost without number that simply leap out at us.

It has been said that truth is stranger than fiction. Certainly that is apparent regarding our text. As we ponder the account, matters that defy our explanation abound, but we read it expectantly.

I recently read a statement made by a seminary classmate of mine with which I concur. He said, "Mysteries are to be studied, but not always understood." I believe that's true, for no one with a finite mind can grasp the complexities of the infinite truths found in the Christmas story.

Probably the first mystery that confronts us centers in the

Characters

found in this story. When God chose people through whom and by whom to work, he chose a nation held in disdain by almost every other nation on earth. Throughout their long history, the Israelites had been persecuted, attacked, opposed, and taken prisoner and held in bondage, as perhaps no other nation. Isn't it strange that God chose Israel as the nation through whom to reveal himself? What a mysterious manner in which to reveal his ways, his laws, and his judgments.

If you and I had written the script for the Christmas story, in all probability we would have seen to it that royalty, or people of great prominence, occupied the leading roles. We would have selected individuals who had worldwide fame, who, when they spoke, could command a vast audience. But when God chose to reveal himself, the characters through whom he made this revelation were plain, ordinary people. The only distinguishing characteristic about Mary and Joseph was their piosity and love for God. Nothing else about them was outstanding. They had done nothing worthy of recognition earlier in their lives; there was nothing about their existence after the birth of Christ that made them stand out in any unusual way. They were plain people, just like you and me.

In the eyes of the world in which they lived, Mary and Joseph were the little, insignificant, harmless people who were most often pushed around by dictators and the like. They were the kind of folk bullies could take great delight in threatening. They had no prestige; they had no influence; they were not close friends with any prominent people who could bring about retaliation against anybody. They had no claim to fame other than the fact that they were people who loved and served God.

With all of the wealthy and influential people of that generation, with the Caesars, the Herods, and others, God chose Mary and Joseph. Through them God manifested his love for all humanity. What a mystery!

Television and movie directors in our day would have cast this drama in a much different fashion. They would have picked out the best known actors and actresses. They would have selected individuals whose names were household words. But when God chose to reveal himself, he moved in a mysterious way.

There's mystery surrounding the characters, but the mystery grows deeper when we remember the

Census

that Luke describes. "In those days, there went out a decree from Caesar Augustus, that all the world should be taxed" (Luke 2:2). Caesar Augustus, of course, was the emperor of the Roman Empire. He decreed that there should be a registration for tax purposes. This move had absolutely no religious significance. To say the least, Rome was areligious, that is, nonreligious. Rome did not support or promote any one religion. Mostly, the Roman Empire was polytheistic.

This Roman decree stated that every man would register in his own hometown. For that reason Mary and Joseph were forced to leave Nazareth to make a very difficult trip down to Bethlehem, Joseph's hometown.

Because of this political move and because of the hand of God working in all of it, the Old Testament Scriptures concerning the birth of the Messiah in Bethlehem were fulfilled and consummated. God took a political maneuver and used it as the backdrop for the greatest spiritual event in human history. All the centuries of prophecy and prediction and promises found in the Old Testament reached their glorious, smashing climax in the most unlikely manner imaginable.

Would you have ever believed that God would take a move politically inspired by a pagan authority, the Roman Empire, and make that a prime cause and factor in his revelation of himself? If you will study the Old Testament closely, you will find that on many occasions God used a pagan nation or pagan individual through whom to reveal himself.

As the first coming of Christ, God moved mysteriously; the second will be the same. We can't predict it. We won't know the day or hour. No one among us knows the mind of God and the way the hand of God moves so he can say, "On this day and on this spot the second coming of Christ will take place." "God moves in mysterious ways his wonders to perform." The census was one of those mysterious ways in which God moved to perform the mystery of the ages.

The plot thickens perceptibly as we move on to reflect on the

Context

in which all of this transpired. The focal point of the entire story is this: God, who is infinite in power, majesty, creative ability, and love, came to earth by means of a human birth. The same divine Architect, whose master plan is revealed in the world and all that is in our universe, chose to reveal himself in the same form as his highest creation, mankind. That's a mystery. We can't understand how infinite God can become finite. We can't grasp how God, 100 percent deity, can reveal himself as a man, 100 percent human, at the same time. This defies our ability to comprehend. The fact of the matter is, this definitely is not the way we would have done it. If you or I had written the script, we would not have revealed infinite power and majesty in a stable.

Satan, during the wilderness temptations of our Lord, made a suggestion far more in keeping with our thoughts. He told Jesus to climb to the pinnacle of the Temple and possibly stand there for a time attracting a big crowd, and when there were thousands of people looking up at him, to jump from the pinnacle of the Temple. Just before he hit the ground he could have a legion or so of angels catch him and spare his life just before being killed by that fall. Satan tempted Jesus with the spectacular and said, "Now, if you really want your kingdom spread around, if you really want the kingdom to come, this is the way to do it." If you and I had written the script, we probably would have followed something far closer to Satan's suggestion than what

God actually did in revealing himself in Bethlehem's barn.

We like the spectacular. We're in love with the bizarre, something that can attract the attention of humanity. We'd blow the trumpets. We'd assemble all the people. We'd have a lot of fanfare and then announce to a vast audience that God's only begotten Son was about to appear. Then we'd draw the curtain and have God's Son occupying the center stage with all of the spotlights on him and make the announcement to the world.

What a mystery it is that God chose to reveal himself in a stable located behind an inn, with no human witnesses other than those involved, and a few dumb animals standing around who could make no verbal comment whatever. It was in such a spot that the infinite God came to earth in the form of a baby. In that poorly illuminated stable, God revealed the mystery of the ages.

Some still seek a rational explanation for the virgin birth. Some still try to figure it out in their own minds. No human can fully grasp it. I cannot stand before you and say I understand God's mysterious revelation in the virgin birth of Jesus Christ. All I can say is that it is the only possible explanation I know for the incarnation, or the way God chose to reveal himself by becoming man and entering into the world. How he did it, I do not know. That he did it, I believe. Jesus was born of a virgin. What a mystery that is.

Remember that we are dealing with the God of creation, the God of power, and the God of love. Remember that the architect is greater than the building, that the God who designed this world and made man in his own image is greater than the world or the man whom he created. The God who set up this world and all that's in our universe both has the right and the ability to supercede the laws by which he governs his material universe. God has complete authority; at any moment he might decide to abridge any or all of the laws that are operative in our world. That he abridged such a law in the coming of Christ is not something I cannot believe. I can believe that the God who made us was capable of doing precisely that, for you see this miracle-working God is still at work. He still is able to accomplish what the world thinks is impossible. He performed a miracle at Bethlehem. It's a miracle that has remained mysterious from that day till this.

Yet there remains another mystery. Mystery surround the characters, the census, and the context of all this, but in my judgment the greatest mystery of all is the

Compassion

of the Creator. The great mystery to me is why God did anything in your behalf and mine.

Man, throughout his history, has spurned God's overtures. Man has consistently done that which is evil in the sight of God. Man has continuously violated God's holy laws. In spite of it, God cared enough to come to this earth in person to prove his love and make known his claims.

When God wanted the world to know all we are capable of knowing about him, he didn't send a prophet. He didn't make a king who would be one of his followers. He didn't call just a nation. When God wanted the highest revelation possible, he came himself! Jesus said, "He that hath seen me hath seen the Father" (John 14:9).

Have you ever in an idle moment asked yourself, I

wonder what God is like? If you have, wonder no more. "He that hath seen me," Jesus said, "hath seen the Father." You want to know what God is like? Look at Jesus Christ as he is portrayed in the Gospels.

There is a real mystery that surrounds God's compassion, for God had nothing to gain from doing what he did in Christ. The only possibility of gain he might realize is found in our response to his offer and the fellowship he can have with us and we can have with him when we yield to the claims of Jesus Christ.

In spite of all that God has done, there are men today like the innkeeper of old who, with a flippant shrug of the shoulder say, "I'm sorry, there's no room." The innkeeper told Joseph there was no vacancy in the inn. Men today flatly state there is no room in their lives for the Lord Jesus. No time for him. No days or hours that they can give to the Lord of all creation.

All over our world men yearn for peace. The angelic hosts spoke of peace to the shepherds on a hillside. There are three kinds of peace: peace with God, peace with one's self, and peace with one's fellowman. May I remind you that it's only when we possess the first two, peace with God and peace with ourselves, that we can live in peace and goodwill toward our fellowman. That peace, which is the only hope for world brotherhood, comes only through faith in the Lord Jesus.

A schoolteacher told of a young boy whom she had taught. He accidentally started a fire in the clothes closet of his home. Fearful of the consequence, he closed the closet door and was so successful in concealing what he had done that the fire was not discovered until too late. The entire house was consumed.

That is a parable of mankind. We try to cover up

our responsibility for sin and refuse the offering of God's love and salvation in Jesus. We destroy the human soul by our rejection of the only offer of help that's ours. My friends, I want to tell you again that the Christmas story is proof positive that God loves you, that his highest desire for you is that you might be saved and possess his peace and the joy of his salvation.